Conter

Wild Dog – Gametrackers, Khwai River Lodge. BOTSWANA

Published by:

Johansens Limited, Therese House, Glasshouse Yard, London EC1A 4JN

Tel: +44 20 7566 9700 Fax: +44 20 7490 2538

Find Johansens on the Internet at www.johansens.com

Production Director:	Daniel Barnett
Production Controller:	Kevin Bradbrook
Production Assistant:	Rachael Gasiorowski
Sub-editor:	Stephanie von Selzam
Senior Designer:	Michael Tompsett
Designers:	Kerri Bennett
	Sue Dixon
Map Illustrations:	Linda Clark
Copywriters:	Norman Flack
	Debra Giles
Manager Southern Africa:	Elane van Rooyen
Inspectors:	Jill Barstow
	Christopher Bonn
	Colin Bridle
	Barbara McMinn
	Sue Partridge
	Bridget Rutherford
	Peter Schaary
Sales and Marketing Manager:	Laurent Martinez
Marketing Executive:	Adam Crabtree
Sales Administrator:	Susan Butterworth
Special Projects Editor:	Fiona Patrick
P.A. to Managing Director:	Joanne Jones
Managing Director:	Andrew Warren

Copyright © 2000 Johansens Limited

Johansens is a member company of Harmsworth Publishing Ltd, a subsidiary of the Daily Mail & General Trust plc

ISBN 1 86017 8073

Printed in England by St Ives plc
Colour origination by Icon Reproduction

Distributed in the UK and Europe by Johnsons International Media Services Ltd, London (direct sales) & Portfolio, Greenford (bookstores). In North America by Hobsons DMI, Cincinnati (direct sales) and Hunter Publishing, New Jersey (bookstores). In Australia and New Zealand by Bookwise International, Findon, South Australia. In Southern Africa by Liquid Amber Distributions, Gillitts, South Africa.

HOW TO USE THIS GUIDE

Our recommendations are presented in alphabetical order by country.

Recommendations within South Africa are presented alphabetically by province. They can be found easily by referring to the contents page.

Illustrated maps precede each section of the guide described above and are intended to provide an indication only of the location of each hotel or game lodge marked by a dot displaying the corresponding page number within the guide.

If you want to find an hotel or game lodge whose name you already know, please refer to the indexes at the back of the guide.

These indexes also include all Johansens recommendations for Great Britain and Ireland 2001 and a section of illustrated listings featuring our recommendations for Europe, North America, Bermuda & The Caribbean and Australia, New Zealand & The Pacific 2001.

Copies of these guides may be purchased directly from Johansens by calling our UK free phone number 0800 269397 or by using the order coupons provided.

Prices throughout the guide are correct at the time of going to press but please check that you understand what the price includes at the time of making a booking.

<u>Caution:</u> We occasionally receive letters from guests who have been charged for accommodation booked in advance but later cancelled. Readers should be aware that by making a reservation with a hotel, either by telephone or in writing, they are enetering into a legal contract. A hotelier under certain circumstances is entitled to make a charge for accommodation when guests fail to arrive, even if notice of the cancellation is given.

Southern African Office:

PO Box 3133, Three Rivers Vereeniging 1939, Gauteng, South Africa

Tel +27 164 549 931 Fax +27 164 548 399

Key to Symbols

White Elephant Lodge, KWAZULU-NATAL, SOUTH AFRICA

14 rms   Total number of rooms

MasterCard accepted

VISA   Visa accepted

AMERICAN EXPRESS accepted

Diners Club accepted

Quiet location

en famille   Guests usually dine together

Access for the disabled

(The 'Access for wheelchairs' symbol (♿) does not necessarily indicate that the property fulfils National Accessible Scheme grading)

M 20   Meeting/conference facilities with maximum number of delegates

8   Children welcome, with minimum age where applicable

Cable/satellite TV in all bedrooms

Fax available in rooms

No-smoking rooms (at least one no-smoking bedroom)

Elevator available for guests' use

Air Conditioning

Outdoor swimming pool

Tennis court at hotel

Croquet lawn at hotel

Fishing can be arranged

Golf course on site or nearby, which has an arrangement with hotel allowing guests to play

Hunting permitted

⑤   Lion, Leopard, Elephant, Rhinoceros and Buffalo can be seen

Game viewing

Bird Watching

Riding can be arranged

Ⓗ   Hotel has a helipad

Airstrip nearby

Licensed for wedding ceremonies

the preferred
champagne
of johansens

Foreword

Mvuu Wilderness Lodge & Camp. LIWONDE NATIONAL PARK, MALAWI

Welcome to the second edition of our Guide to Southern Africa. You will have noticed that we have added 'Country Houses' to this title in recognition of the many smaller country properties that would not wish to be described as an 'hotel'.

Our team of inspectors have spent the past twelve months revisiting the hotels and game lodges that we recommended last year and inspecting new establishments for consideration in this, the 2001, edition. We are delighted to welcome new recommendations from both Malawi and Zambia in this edition.

To maintain and monitor standards, we encourage constructive comments and observations through the 'Guest Survey Forms' printed at the back of this guide. This information is invaluable, and whether it contains criticism or praise, we are always pleased to hear from you.

Our first Guide to 'Recommended Hotels & Lodges – Australia, New Zealand, The Pacific' is also published this year, which means that Johansens now recommend over 1500 Hotels, Country Houses, Traditional Inns, Game Lodges and Business Meeting Venues throughout four continents.

Order forms to purchase all Johansens titles are provided at the back of this guide together with a list of our other recommendations which can also be found by location or 'keyword' search on our website: www.johansens.com.

Direct reservations can be made on our website and many recommendations display a 'Call Free Now' facility enabling you to speak directly to the hotel at no cost to yourself.

We very much hope that you appreciate our recommendations for 2001 as much as you have enjoyed using our guides in the past.

Finally, you will discover that to mention Johansens when you arrange your booking and again when you arrive, will make you a most welcome guest.

Andrew Warren,
Managing Director

ECO MAP OF SOUTHERN AFRICA

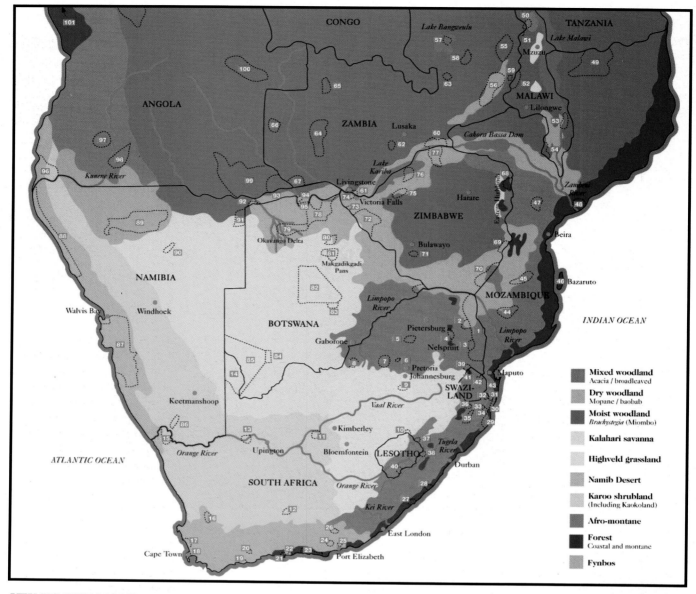

Mixed woodland
Acacia / broadleaved

Dry woodland
Mopane / baobab

Moist woodland
Brachystegia (Miombo)

Kalahari savanna

Highveld grassland

Namib Desert

Karoo shrubland
(Including Kaokoland)

Afro-montane

Forest
Coastal and montane

Fynbos

KEY TO THE MOST IMPORTANT NATIONAL PARKS AND NATURE RESERVES IN SOUTHERN AFRICA

SOUTH AFRICA
1. Kruger National Park
2. Klaserie-Timbavati Nature Reserve
3. Sabi-Sands Nature Reserve
4. Blyde River Canyon Nature Reserve
5. Morekele National Park
6. Borakalalo Nature Reserve
7. Pilanesberg National Park
8. Madikwe Game Reserve
9. Suikerbosrand Nature Reserve
10. Golden Gate National Park
11. Vaalbos National Park
12. Karoo National Park
13. Augrabies National Park
14. Kalahari Gemsbok National Park
15. Richtersveld National Park
16. Tankwa-Karoo National Park
17. West Coast National Park
18. Cape Point Nature Reserve
19. De Hoop Nature Reserve
20. Bontebok National Park
21. Wilderness National Park
22. Knysna Lakes Park
23. Tsitsikamma National Park
24. Zuurberg National Park
25. Addo Elephant National Park
26. Mountain Zebra National Park
27. Dwesa Nature Reserve
28. Mkambati Nature Reserve
29. Lake St Lucia Wetland Park

30. Maputaland Coastal Reserve
31. Tembe Elephant Reserve
32. Ndumo Game Reserve
33. Mkuze Game Reserve
34. Phinda Resource Reserve
35. Hluhluwe-Umfolozi Game Reserve
36. Itala Game Reserve
37. Royal Natal Game Reserve
38. Giant's Castle Game Reserve
39. Songimvelo Nature Reserve

LESOTHO
40. Sehlabathebe National Park

SWAZILAND
41. Mlilwane and Malolotja Nature Reserves
42. Hlane Royal National Park and Mkhaya Game Reserve

MOZAMBIQUE
43. Maputo Elephant Reserve
44. Banhine National Park
45. Zinhave National Park
46. Bazaruto Archipelago National Park
47. Gorongosa National Park
48. Marromeu National Park
49. Niassa National Park

MALAWI
50. Nyika Plateau National Park

51. Vwaza Marsh Game Reserve
52. Kasungu National Park
53. Liwonde-Lake Malawi National Park
54. Lengwe National Park

ZAMBIA
55. North Luangwa National Park
56. South Luangwa National Park
57. Isangano National Park
58. Lavushi Manda National Park
59. Lukusuzi National Park
60. Lower Zambezi National Park
61. Mosi-oa-tunya National Park
62. Lochinvar National Park
63. Kasanka National Park
64. Kafue National Park
65. West Lunga National Park
66. Liuwa Plain National Park
67. Sloma Ngwezi National Park

ZIMBABWE
68. Nyanga National Park
69. Chimanimani National Park
70. Gonarezhou National Park
71. Matobo National Park
72. Hwange National Park
73. Kazuma Pan National Park
74. Zambezi-Victoria Falls National Park
75. Chizarira National Park
76. Matusadona National Park

77. Mana Pools National Park

BOTSWANA
78. Chobe National Park
79. Moremi Game Reserve
80. Nxai Pan National Park
81. Makgadikgadi Pan National Park
82. Central Kalahari Game Reserve
83. Khutse Game Reserve
84. Mabuasehube Game Reserve
85. Gemsbok National Park

NAMIBIA
86. Fish River Canyon Park
87. Namib-Naukluft National Park
88. Skeleton Coast National Park
89. Etosha National Park
90. Waterberg Plateau National Park
91. Kaudom National Park
92. Mahango Game Reserve
93. Caprivi Game Park
94. Mudumo National Park
95. Mamili National Park

ANGOLA
96. Iona National Park
97. Bicuari National Park
98. Mupa National Park
99. Cuando Cubango Public Park Complex
100. Cameia National Park
101. Quiçama National Park

BIOMES OF SOUTHERN AFRICA

The variety of landforms and vegetation zones, or biomes, has resulted in a remarkably high diversity of species in southern Africa.

The Eco Map and its accompanying text on biomes were compiled by Duncan Butchart. © Wilderness Safaris 1993. (Updated by Duncan Butchart, 1995.) The information is adapted from Southern African Biomes by M C Rutherford and R H Westfall (Memoirs of the Botanical Survey of South Africa: 54, Pretoria, 1986) and The Vegetation Map of Africa by F White (Unesco, Paris, 1983).

Map courtesy of Duncan Butchart–Wildernes Safaris.

MIXED WOODLAND

Type of savanna characterised by relatively short trees, including Acacia and broad-leaved species. Also referred to as bushveld. Generally occurring at altitudes below 1 500 m, it includes much of the lowveld. Wide diversity of species, but few are restricted to this biome.

NAMIB DESERT

Occurs along the western seaboard north of the Orange River, below 400 m. Exceptionally arid climate (less than 100 mm per annum) creates a true desert with giant sand dunes and succulent flora. Many species are restricted to this biome including the living fossil plant Welwitschia.

DRY WOODLAND

Dominated by Mopane trees and shrubs and is typical of low-lying areas and river valleys below 1 000 m. Baobab trees are often common in this type of savanna. Soils are usually clay based and seasonal pans are a feature. Wide diversity of species, but few are restricted to this biome.

KAROO SHRUBLAND

Semi-desert, mostly below 1 000 m in the dry west. Dominated by shrubs, grasses and succulents. Rugged in parts, with canyons and valleys. Few perennial rivers. Many species are restricted to this zone. Includes Kaokoland, Damaraland, Richtersveld and Namaqualand.

MOIST WOODLAND

Also known as Miombo, this savanna type is dominated by Brachystegia and Julbernardia trees which often form a closed canopy. Occurs above 1 000 m. Does not support great numbers of large mammals, but several species of birds are restricted to this biome.

AFRO-MONTANE

Grassland and heath above 1 500 m and up to 3 000 m. Mostly along the crest of the Drakensberg. Rugged countryside with erratic but generally high rainfall. Several species are restricted to this biome in southern Africa, but also occur in the Rift Valley and Ethiopian Highlands.

KALAHARI SAVANNA

Very open terrain dominated by grassland with scattered trees and shrubs. Very deep sands underlie the vegetation. Occurs below 1 000 m and receives less than 400 mm rain per annum. Fossil dunes, dry river valleys and salt pans. No surface water. Hyphaene palms in the north.

FOREST

Dominated by large evergreen trees, forests contain few mammals but many birds. Coastal and lowland forests occur along the eastern seaboard, while montane forest occurs in pockets about 1 200 m. High rainfall is a feature. Only small fragments of true closed-canopy forest remain.

HIGHVELD GRASSLAND

Flat or hilly areas largely devoid of trees except along water courses. Dominant vegetation type at altitudes above 1 500 m. Cold dry winters render this biome particularly prone to fire and frost which prohibit the growth of most trees.

FYNBOS

Restricted to the south-western Cape, and one of the world's six floral kingdoms. Generally hilly or mountainous country, dominated by proteas, heaths, restios and bulbous plants. Receives rainfall in winter only. A great number of species are restricted to this zone.

An Insurance Policy designed for Peace of Mind

Marsh Leisure Group, part of the Marsh and McLennan Companies, the world's leading Risk Management and Financial Services group, is proud to continue as the Preferred Professional Services Partner to Johansens Recommendations, properties and guests worldwide.

At Marsh Leisure Group, we realise that time is probably your most valuable commodity and that on matters like insurance, you need peace of mind in the knowledge that such an important issue is in the right hands.

For over 20 years, we have provided a comprehensive range of insurance and financial services for our clients operating Hotels, Inns, Restaurants, Country Houses and Holiday Cottages. These embrace all aspects for which protection and security may be required.

With an experienced and professional team able to offer sound advice, we believe we are ideally placed to service those establishments meeting the high standards required for entry in a Johansens Guide.

Please contact:

Brian Blake _____ 002711 506 5000

Contact Marsh for your business insurance requirements at:

The Marsh Centre
88 Grayston Drive
Sandton
South Africa

Tel: +2711 506 51 73
Fax: +2711 506 53 40

MARSH
An *MMC* Company

BOTSWANA

GAMETRACKERS - KHWAI RIVER LODGE

PO BOX 786432, SANDTON 2146, SOUTH AFRICA
TEL: 27 11 481 6052 FAX: 27 11 481 6065 E-MAIL: gtres@iafrica.com

Gametracker safari camps allow visitors an insight into real Africa, without sacrificing comfort. In a sparsely populated and remote region which remains largely untouched by modern hands, each lodge has developed an active role in environmental protection, investing a great deal in community relations with the local Botswana people. Enjoying settings within three diverse eco-systems, the camps offer spacious individual luxury tents, all air conditioned, and built of timber and canvas. Each camp, including Savute Elephant Camp and Eagle Island Camp at Xaxaba, boast en suite facilities, elegant four-poster beds and have private wooden viewing decks. Excellent cuisine helps sustain visitors on the wide array of activities available. Game drives, guided walks, sundowner cruises, birdwatching and game flights on request in light aircraft provide numerous encounters with an astonishing array of wildlife. Opportunities abound to view lions, leopards, cheetah, wildebeest, wild dogs, hippos, pelicans, storks, and of course, elephants, from close range. After a dusty day in the wilderness, guests can retire back to base and cool off with a swim (heated pools), watch the sun go down to a chorus of frog chants before dining al fresco. **Directions:** By air charter from Maun. Price guide: Rooms US$400–500 per person.

MALAWI

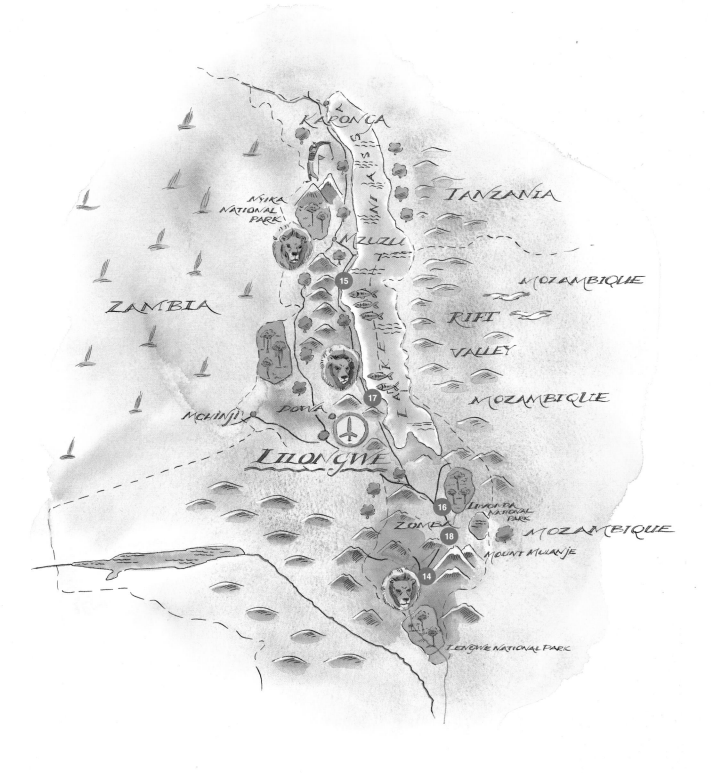

MOUNT SOCHE HOTEL

GLYN JONES ROAD, PO BOX 284, BLANTYRE, MALAWI
TEL: 265 620 588 FAX: 265 620 154 E-MAIL: msh@sdmp.org.mw

Built in the 1970s, this is Malawi's leading hotel. Ideally situated in the centre of Blantyre it has a high reputation for its service, comfort and hospitality. Manager Paul Dalrymple, who has extensive experience from working in major hotels throughout Britain, has been supervising a refurbishment programme to introduce even more comfort and elegance to the interior, combined with 21st century high-tech facilities. The 134 en suite bedrooms are individually and attractively furnished and well equipped. Each is air-conditioned and facilities include five-channel digital satellite TV, telephone, radio and taped music and electric power points. The hotel takes pride in its excellent cuisine with menus offering a good variety of international dishes in the elegant 5th-floor restaurant, complemented by a wide selection of fine wines. Guests can relax in the hotel's attractive gardens or make use of the swimming pool. Golf, tennis, and squash facilities are nearby. The surrounding countryside is one of infinite variety and for those who want to explore and soak up the African experience there are regular excursions to Lengwe National National Park, the Zomba Plateau, Mount Mulanje and tea estates. Mount Soche is also an excellent venue for business visitors; its conference and meetings facilities are the best in Malawi. **Directions:** Available on request. Price guide: Room rates available on request.

CHINTHECHE INN

PO BOX 9, CHINTHECHE, MALAWI
TEL: 265 357 211 FAX: 265 357 246 E-MAIL: chininn@malawi.net

Chintheche Inn stands on the spectacular northern shores of Lake Malawi, a beautiful position, which combines with the myriad exotic fish and astonishing variety of birds to create a very special atmosphere. Restful and unfussy, its comfortable en suite rooms open onto the white sandy beach, where guests can enjoy swimming, excellent snorkelling, windsurfing or sailing, and trips in traditional wooden fishing boats. Dining is al fresco with a warm welcome extended by the Manager's wife Deidre, an enthusiastic cook. Land based activities include superb bird watching and there are many nearby places to visit such as Likoma Island, Mkuwazi Forest, and for those with an interest in local history, the site of Bandawe Church,

one of Central Africa's earliest mission stations. Unique amongst the Wilderness Collection, and very reasonably priced, Chintheche Inn epitomises the ideal hideaway for those who appreciate well organised simplicity. Remote, yet accessible, it provides the perfect antidote to the stresses of city life or a welcome resting point between long and dusty safaris. **Directions:** Access to the Inn is by road from Lilongwe or Mzuzu. From Lilongwe travel 125km east to Salima, then 277km north to Chintheche. From Mzuzu travel 48km east to Nkhata Bay, then 45km south to Chintheche. Visitors can also fly by private charter to the nearby airstrip. Price guide (half-board): Single US$100; double/twin US$150.

Mvuu Wilderness Lodge & Camp, Liwonde National Park

CENTRAL AFRICAN WILDERNESS SAFARIS, PO BOX 489, LILONGWE, MALAWI
TEL: 265 771 393 FAX: 265 771 397 E-MAIL: info@wilderness.malawi.net

This lodge and camp offer visitors seclusion, peace and a superb wilderness experience in one of Malawi's finest reserves. Elephant, waterbuck, sable and impala drink and bathe in the waters of the Shire River which flows through the superb Liwonde National Park; lion, leopard and kudu roam inland. Lovebirds, the Brownbreasted Barbet, Pel's Fishing Owl and the Palmut Vulture are among more than 370 species of birds winging overhead. Mvuu Camp Wilderness Lodge offers accommodation for a maximum of 10 guests in four luxury tents and one superb honeymoon suite. In addition to a bar and excellent dining area, the lodge's fully inclusive service includes exciting river safaris and adventurous bush walks and game drives.

Experienced guides are on hand to help guests who wish to see elephants enjoying the cool river waters or who want to learn about the surrounding flora and fauna. A maximum of 26 guests at Mvuu Camp sleep in twin-bedded tents overlooking the Shire River. There is a choice of self-catering facilities or an open-air restaurant and bar from where hippo and crocodiles can be viewed in the river. Hot and cold showers and ablution facilities are available for those who prefer to camp. **Directions:** From Lilongwe (230kms) or Blantyre (123kms) turn east off the main road between the two just south of Liwonde. At the crossroads turn right, cross a railway line and follow the signs. Price guide: Rooms $130–$270 incl. all meals and game activities.

LIVINGSTONIA BEACH HOTEL

PO BOX 11, SALIMA, CENTRAL REGION, MALAWI
TEL: 265 263 222/444 FAX: 265 263 452 E-MAIL: livingst.hotel@comw.net

With its large expanse of golden sands edged by palms and natural mature woodland, Livingstonia Beach Hotel is an oasis for the holidaymaker seeking complete relaxation and a secluded haven in which to enjoy watersports, explore and soak up the exciting atmosphere and essence of Africa. It is a traditional hotel surrounded by colourful gardens standing on the edge of Lake Malawi. For many years it has been recognised as being one of the best run lake resorts, offering comfort, warm hospitality and friendly, individual and unobtrusive service. Recent investment and refurbishment has increased the hotel's already high standard. The delightfully furnished and gracious en suit guest accommodation has every facility from air conditioning to satellite television and telephone. Excellent, imaginatively prepared meals are enjoyed in a stylish, cool dining room, whilst less formal meals are available at the bar. While escape from the bustle of everyday life is paramount, the more active guests can take part in numerous sporting activities including lawn tennis, beach volleyball, swimming, sailing, canoeing, scuba diving and fishing. Excursions can be arranged to Hammer Peak, View Point, Cape Maclear and the Mua Mission. **Directions:** Minibus transfer from Lilongwe airport. Price guide: Single US$115–US$140; double/twin US$72.50–US$85; suite US$88.33–US$150 per person.

KU CHAWE INN

PO BOX 71, ZOMBA, MALAWI
TEL: 265 522 566 FAX: 265 522 509

Ku Chawe Inn stands 3,000 feet high above the morning mists on the edge of the Zomba Plateau overlooking the historic, former capital of Malawi, . Surrounded by terraces of beautiful landscaped gardens, this regal hotel offers guests magnificent views towards the Shire Highlands, majestic Mount Mulanje and beyond. The plateau is a tranquil forest reserve renowned for its temperate climate and natural splendour. Among its lush pine forests there are meandering rivers, foaming waterfalls, wild orchids and brightly coloured butterflies. No expense has been spared in making the Inn a comfortable, welcoming and cool retreat. The bedrooms are all en suite, tastefully decorated and furnished and have every modern convenience from satellite television to radio and telephone. Each also has an open fireplace and splendid views of Lake Chirwa, shimmering in the distance. Superb cuisine is served in the stylish restaurant whose surroundings are reminiscent of an Alpine ski lodge. Dinner choice is from an imaginative à la carte menu or an extensive buffet carvery. In winter, diners are warmed by a large open fire in the middle of the restaurant and bar. Guests can relax amid the exquisite beauty of Ku Chawe's gardens or, when feeling active, visit the Mandala and William Falls, the nearby botanical gardens or the Parliament Buildings in Zomba.
Directions: North east from Blantyre along M3. Price guide: Available on request.

MAURITIUS

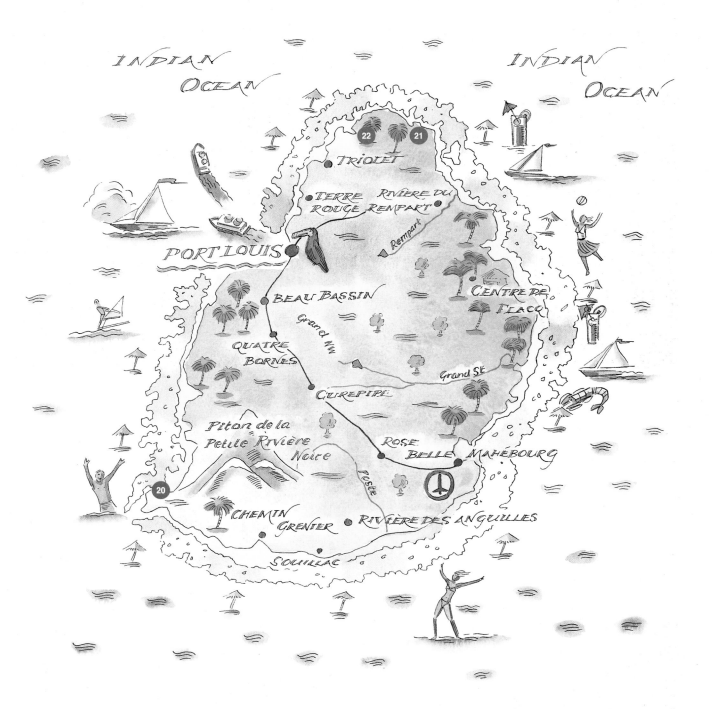

INDIAN OCEAN

INDIAN OCEAN

22 21

TRIOLET

TERRE ROUGE

RIVIÈRE DU REMPART

Rempart

PORT LOUIS

BEAU BASSIN

CENTRE DE FLACQ

Grand NW

QUATRE BORNES

Grand SE

CUREPIPE

Piton de la Petite Rivière Noire

ROSE BELLE

MAHEBOURG

Poste

20

CHEMIN GRENIER

RIVIÈRE DES ANGUILLES

SOUILLAC

PARADIS

MAURITIUS HOUSE, 1 PORTSMOUTH ROAD, GUILDFORD, SURREY GU2 4BL
RESERVATIONS TEL: +44 1483 533008 FAX: +44 1483 532820 E-MAIL: b@bctuk.demon.co.uk

Occupying the 125 acre private peninsula of Le Morre on the south westerly tip of the island, the appropriately named Paradis is an oasis for the sports-loving holidaymaker. Sprawled between Le Morne mountains and the Indian ocean, this exclusive hideaway possesses a golf course of international renown and offers a myriad of water sports including waterskiing, wind-surfing, diving and deep sea fishing. In addition there are tennis and squash courts and two fresh water pools. Visitors of a less active persuasion may laze on the never ending golden beaches that flank the hotel, or bask in the exotic fragrances of the tropical gardens. The large, well-aired and beautifully-furnished rooms are of a typically Mauritian design. Visitors can choose to have either a peerless view of the Indian Ocean, or breathtaking vistas of the imposing Morne mountain. The Paradis prides itself on the quality of its cuisine. The four excellent restaurants offer a choice of Italian, themed buffets and creole styles, all of which unleash the succulent flavours of the local seafood. After dinner, guests can relax in the easy opulence of the hotel's three bars and enjoy the resident cabaret. Attractions in the vicinity include the Grand Basin, Casela Bird Park and the Black River Gorge. **Directions:** Transfers are available from the airport. Price guide: Rooms £202–£588.

PARADISE COVE

ANSE LA RAIE, MAURITIUS
TEL: 230 204 4000 FAX: 230 204 4040 E-MAIL: Pcove@intnet.mu

Superbly located in lush tropical gardens, this is an ideal, intimate holiday hideaway. Built in traditional Mauritian style around a private and secluded cove, this superb hotel overlooks clear blue waters with scenic views to the distant northern islands. The white sanded cove is the ideal place to relax and enjoy peace and tranquillity. Sixty seven deluxe rooms and suites are elegantly furnished and decorated. Each is en suite and fitted with every amenity expected by today's discerning traveller, from air-conditioning and TV to electronic safe and mini-bar. All face seawards and have either a terrace or balcony and direct access to the beach. Two restaurants, a beach bar and a poolside bar offer a choice of formal and informal dining with the emphasis on fresh produce, seafood and exotic cuisine. La Belle Creole is the main restaurant where guests can enjoy panoramic views. La Cocoteraie offers a more casual setting with seating under thatched pavilions along the shoreline. The Beach Bar specialises in lunchtime grills, and Le Cozy Corner with lounge and terrace beside the hotel's magnificent pool is popular for snacks, pre-dinner cocktails and end of evening cultural shows. For the energetic, there are floodlit tennis courts, a gym and a wide range of watersports. Catamaran cruises and under sea walks are free of charge. **Directions:** Transfers are available from the airport, 60km away. Price guide: Single US$265–US$290; double/twin US$230–US$390; suite US$310–US$505.

ROYAL PALM

MAURITIUS HOUSE, 1 PORTSMOUTH ROAD, GUILDFORD, SURREY GU2 4BL
RESERVATIONS TEL: +44 1483 533008 FAX: +44 1483 532820 E-MAIL: b@bctuk.demon.co.uk

Perched on a sweeping bend of the exquisite Grand Sable beach, the Royal Palm is unquestionably one the most chic and comfortable hotels on the Indian Ocean. This luxuriant hideaway is the briefest stroll away from the fashionable Grand Bay, which offers first-class shops, a local market and interesting churches. With staff outnumbering guests by three to one, a tranquil and indulgent stay is guaranteed. While escape from the bustle of everyday life is paramount, the more active guest can take advantage of the numerous sporting facilities that the Royal Palm provides. As Mauritius boasts some of the clearest and most luminous waters in the world, guests will want to sail, fish, snorkel and dive in this tropical idyll. The food is truly magnificent. The Royal Palm has two first class restaurants presided over by culinary maestro Richard Ekkebus, who infuses the magnificent local seafood with the flavours of Europe and the Indian Ocean. The Royal Palm's rooms and suites are exquisitely furnished and exude a gracious and stately elegance. The 'Royal Suite', a private three bedroom luxury suite at the heart of the hotel, has attracted many crowned heads of state and world leaders. **Directions:** Transfers are available from the airport, by road 1hr 10mins. 47 miles by main road from airport to Grand Bay. Price guide (per person): Rooms £158–£1045.

MOZAMBIQUE

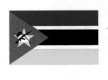

BENGUERRA LODGE

RESERVATIONS: BENGUELA ISLAND HOLIDAYS, 89 HOUGHTON DRIVE, HOUGHTON 2041, JOHANNESBURG
TEL: 27 11 483 2734 FAX: 27 11 728 3767 E-MAIL: benguela@icon.co.za

Accessible by boat and air, the thatched Benguerra Lodge offers discerning visitors complete seclusion on a languid and private island off Mozambique's famed coastline. The lodge commands awe-inspiring views of Benguerra Bay's golden beaches and coral reefs and is flanked by an idyllic forest of acacia and milkwood trees. The tropical gardens are imaginatively designed and populated by an abundant and colourful bird life, with 125 species of birds to be viewed on the island. Built entirely from local materials so as to blend into the natural surroundings, each of the en suite chalets has its own immaculate view of the Indian Ocean. With a Portuguese motif, the food is flamboyantly prepared. Befitting a tropical island hideaway, the chef specialises in fresh seafood and the calamari, prawns and crab should not be missed. The lodge is an oasis for snorkellers and divers, with the unpolluted water providing the clearest views of breathtaking coral reef and a stupefying array of fish. For the more adventurous, Benguerra Lodge has four 22-foot boats fully equipped for big game fishing, while trips on customised fly fishing boats can also be organised. **Directions:** The lodge is accessible by air from Johannesburg to Vilanculos, which is a short boat trip from Benguerra Bay. Price guide: Rooms US$235–US$285 per person.

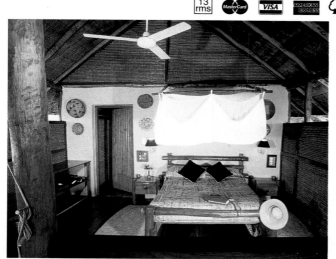

SEA VIEW

PO BOX 373, LÜDERITZ, NAMIBIA
TEL: 264 63 20 34 11 FAX: 264 63 20 34 14 E-MAIL: michaels@ldz.namib.com

This award-winning hotel stands in a quiet residential area of the picturesque harbour town of Lüderitz with superb views over the harbour and bay. The town was founded in 1883 and is a splendid example of German architecture. German owner Ingrid Morgan and her daughter offer a most hospitable welcome and maintain the standards of the hotel at an extremely high level. Décor and furniture throughout are attractive, relaxing and comfortable. The 22 bedrooms are tastefully furnished and have en suite bathrooms with either bath or shower. 19 of the rooms have panoramic sea or town views from their balconies. All provide guests with every modern comfort, including television, radio, direct line telephone, coffee and tea-making facilities. Guests can absorb breathtaking sunsets while sipping pre-dinner drinks in the cosy lounge before enjoying the à la carte delights in the attractive restaurant. Chef Johannes Aaron specialises in imaginative seafood dishes. A braai area overlooks the sea. The hotel's heated indoor swimming pool is a popular venue and for those who like watersports, Agate Beach is within easy reach. Excursions can be arranged to the ghost mining town of Kolmanskop, the former diamond settlements of Bogenfels and Pomono and Halifax Island to view the penguin colony. **Directions:** The hotel is 816km south-west of Windhoek. From town entrance, turn right into Woermann Street. Price guide: Single N\$335; double/twin N\$530.

SAM'S GIARDINO HOTEL

PO BOX 1401, SWAKOPMUND, NAMIBIA
TEL: +264 64 403 210 FAX +264 64 403 500 E-MAIL: samsart@iafrica.com.na

This small hotel is situated in the heart of a fascinating little seaside town of traditional buildings bounded by desert sands on Namibia's Atlantic Coast. It offers superb hospitality with nothing too much trouble for Swiss-born owner and master hotelier Samuel Egger. Service is exemplary and comfort for guests excellent. Inside and out, Sam's Giardino Hotel is typically modern Swiss. Neat, tidy and tasteful with more than just a touch of 21st century style and elegance combined with charm and tranquillity. Each bedroom is delightfully furnished with every comfort and facility to satisfy the most discerning guest. There is a cosy bar and library and a superb restaurant where the chef proprietor prepares the finest Mediterranean gourmet cuisine, complemented by a first-class selection of wines. Guests relish his cheese fondue, pre and after dinner drinks in the hotel's extensive garden. For the connoisseur and amateur alike there are weekly wine tastings and smokers' nights where a good cigar can be enjoyed with a class of port and a plate of cheese. The town's main shopping area is just a short stroll away and the more adventurous can participate in arranged desert excursions. **Directions:** On entering Swakopmund from Usakos turn left at the traffic lights, turn left again at the second junction and after approximately 200 metres on the right side in Lazarett Street. Price guide: Single R400; double/twin R475–R640.

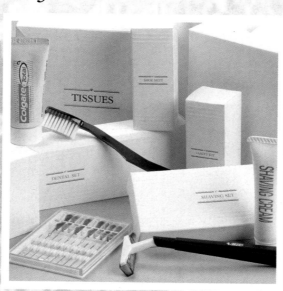

SEYCHELLES

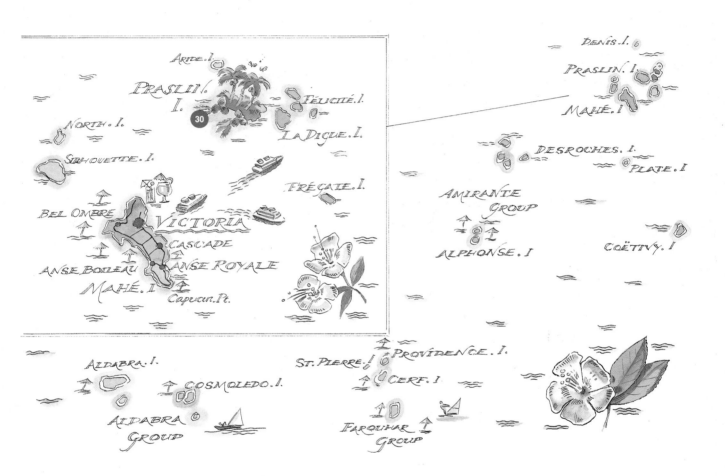

ARIDE. I.

PRASLIN.
I.

NORTH . I.

SILHOUETTE . I.

BEL OMBRE

VICTORIA

CASCADE

ANSE BOILEAU   ANSE ROYALE

MAHÉ . I.   Capucin . Pt.

FÉLICITÉ. I.

LA DIGUE . I.

FRÉGATE . I.

DENIS . I.

PRASLIN . I.

MAHÉ . I.

DESROCHES . I.

PLATE . I

AMIRANTE
GROUP

ALPHONSE . I

COËTIVY . I

ALDABRA . I.

COSMOLEDO . I.

ALDABRA
GROUP

ST. PIERRE . I

PROVIDENCE . I.

CERF . I

FARQUHAR
GROUP

SEYCHELLES COUSINE ISLAND

PO BOX 67404, BRAYNSTON, 2021 GAUTENG
TEL: 27 11 706 3104 FAX: 27 11 706 4752

Rising from clear, turquoise Indian Ocean waters a few degrees south of the equator and approximately 1,500 miles east of Africa, Cousine is a small island paradise of lush vegetation fringed with a beautiful, unspoilt white beach. It is a private nature reserve and home to five of the Seychelles endemic bird species. A maximum of ten guests share the island with its numerous wildlife inhabitants. Accommodation is in four spacious, air-conditioned villas built in old French colonial style. They are positioned to ensure maximum privacy amongst the natural undergrowth of casuarina trees just 30 metres from the pristine beach. Each has every comfort and luxury and superb sea and mountain views. There are front and rear patios, a spacious bedroom,

dressing room, lounge, bathroom with Jacuzzi and double shower, refrigerator, ice machine, ceiling fan, satellite television, video, CD/cassette player, telephone, electronic safe, bathrobes and slippers. Excellent meals are served in your villa or in the air-conditioned restaurant of the main Pavilion. This also houses an attractive lounge, well-stocked library and cocktail bar and overlooks a large freshwater swimming pool and the beach. A resident conservation officer is on hand to advise on the island life. Diving and snorkelling safaris and visits to neighbouring islands can be arranged. **Directions:** By helicopter from Mahe. Price guide (fully inclusive): US$1,350–US$1,450. Helicopter US$460 per person return flight.

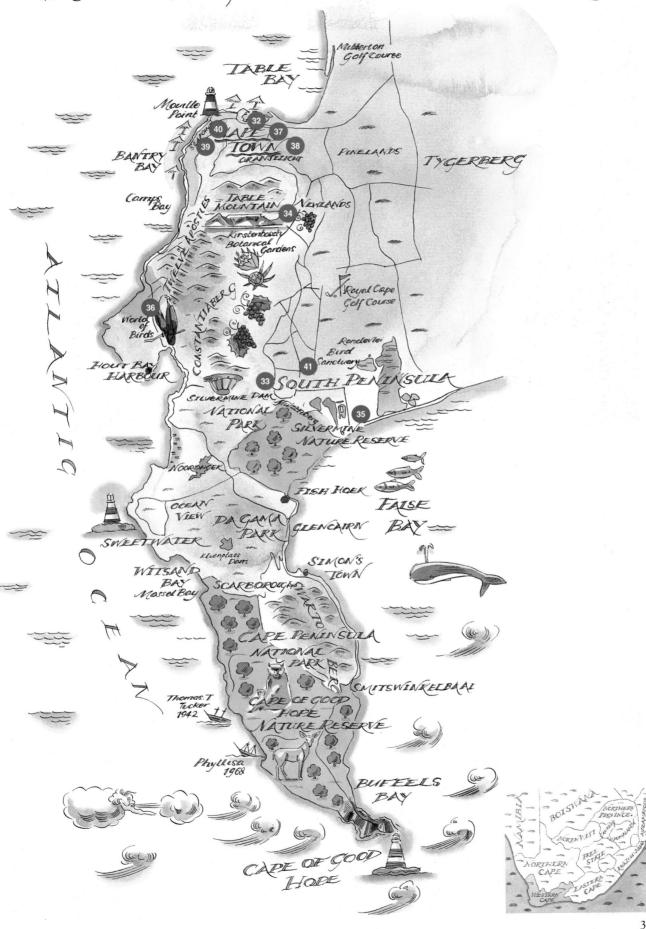

SOUTH AFRICA
CAPE TOWN / CAPE PENINSULA

Mulberton Golf Course

TABLE BAY

Moulle Point

32

Seapoint **40** Cape **37**

39 TOWN **38**

ORANJEZICHT

BANTRY BAY

PINELANDS

TYGERBERG

Camps Bay

TABLE MOUNTAIN

Newlands **34**

Kirstenbosch Botanical Gardens

TWELVE APOSTLES

Royal Cape Golf Course

36

World of Birds

CONSTANTIABERG

Rondevlei Bird Sanctuary

Hout Bay Harbour

41

33 SOUTH PENINSULA

Silvermine Dam

NATIONAL PARK

Steenberg

SILVERMINE **35**

NATURE RESERVE

Noordhoek

FISH HOEK

FALSE BAY

OCEAN VIEW

DA GAMA PARK

GLENCAIRN

SWEETWATER

Kleinplaas Dam

SIMON'S TOWN

WITSAND BAY

Massel Bay

SCARBOROUGH

CAPE PENINSULA

NATIONAL PARK

BERG

SMITSWINKELBAAI

Thomas T. Tucker 1942

CAPE OF GOOD HOPE

NATURE RESERVE

Phyllisia 1968

BUFFELS BAY

CAPE OF GOOD HOPE

ATLANTIC

OCEAN

NAMIBIA

BOTSWANA

NORTHERN PROVINCE

NORTH WEST

GAUTENG

MPUMALANGA

FREE STATE

KWAZULU NATAL

NORTHERN CAPE

EASTERN CAPE

WESTERN CAPE

CAPE GRACE

WEST QUAY, VICTORIA AND ALFRED WATERFRONT, CAPE TOWN
TEL: 27 21 410 7100 FAX: 27 21 419 7622 E-MAIL: reservations@capegrace.com

Surrounded by water on three sides, Cape Grace creates the illusion of an elegant luxury liner moored to the West Quay. Once aboard, the illusion continues with views of Table Mountain, the busy harbour and yacht marina also enjoyed from the guestrooms. Built in a contemporary French classical style, reflecting the architecture of Cape Town itself, there is a seamless transition from old to new creating a sense of vibrancy reflected by the bright fresh décor. The service is of a very high standard, achieved with a purposefulness and efficiency by multilingual staff who genuinely care about their guests. Quay West restaurant is uncluttered and airy, serving modern interpretations of classic dishes. Afternoon tea and cakes and Sunday brunches are also available. All guest rooms and suites have separate dressing rooms, walk in showers, double vanity bathrooms and generous lounge areas. Some have private balconies and others have facilities for the disabled. 20 new loft rooms have been added o the top floor. Guests can enjoy complimentary access to a nearby health club. Shops, museums, restaurants and the aquarium are just a short walk from the hotel. Table Mountain, Signal Hill and the Kirstenbosch Botanical Gardens are a short taxi ride away.**Directions:** 20 minutes drive from Cape Town international airport. Price guide (inc. VAT and full English breakfast): Single R1885– R2480; double R1990–R2585; apartments and suites R3810–R7180.

SÉRÉNITÉ WELLNESS CENTRE

16 DEBAREN CLOSE, CONSTANTIA, CAPE TOWN
TEL: 27 21 713 1760 FAX: 27 21 713 0049 E-MAIL: info@serenite.co.za

Since opening in 1998, the Sérénité Wellness Centre has established itself as one of South Africa's leading health and beauty spas. Set in the lush forests of Cape Town's Constantia Valley, the Centre effortlessly combines five star indulgence with the very best in holistic treatments. Superbly trained staff and the latest technology ensure that service is of the highest standard, and experts in each field, including a medical doctor, fitness consultant and dietician are on hand to create individual, personalised programmes. From Advanced Beauty Therapy to Eastern techniques such as Yoga and Tai Chi, all visitors will find something to experience and enjoy. Otherwise they can take a relaxing swim in one of three pools, benefit from a leisurely game of tennis, or admire spectacular views stretching as far as Table Mountain and False Bay. There are golf and horse riding facilities nearby, and a meditational retreat is set aside in the tranquil gardens for those seeking a more solitary respite from the stresses of the outside world. Luxury and attention to detail bombard the senses in each of the elegant guest suites. Fresh fruit, flowers and bathgowns are replaced daily, while mahogany beds and down-feather duvets provide maximum comfort. A stunning Presidential suite is available upon request. The Centre is also extremely proud of its delicious but healthy cuisine. **Directions:** Travel to the Centre by the N2 road. Price guide (full-board & all treatments): R1,000 per person per day.

THE VINEYARD HOTEL

COLINTON ROAD, NEWLANDS 7700, WESTERN CAPE
TEL: 27 21 683 3044 FAX: 27 21 683 3365 E-MAIL:hotel@vineyard.co.za

The landscaped gardens of stinkwood, coral and indigenous trees create a natural mantle extending to six acres around The Vineyard Hotel. Bordered by the Liesbeeck river and facing Devil's Peak it is easy to see why such a beautiful place was chosen by Lady Anne Barnard as her home in 1800. Today this well-run hotel is owned by the Petousis family and exudes the warmth of a large family home in the style of its illustrious past. Its owner favours the murals of South African ceramicist Esias Bosch for impressive contemporary decoration. There are two restaurants: 'Au Jardin', which is independently managed by a French chef and was recently rated as one of the best ten restaurants in South Africa, enjoys a panoramic view of the gardens and Devil's Peak through huge glass panels. The 'Courtyard' restaurant has a simpler style and offers a surprising choice of excellent dishes. A fully equipped gym faces the garden, adjacent to a heated swimming pool for exercise or recreation. Eight suites and two garden cottages are included in the 160 well equipped and comfortable bedrooms, most of which have either mountain or courtyard views. The all new 'Vineyard Conference Centre' boasts two completely dedicated floors, tailormade for conferences and weddings. **Directions:** Approximately 20 minutes from Cape Town International Airport via the N2 motorway. Price guide: Rooms R535–R2250.

COLONA CASTLE

PO BOX 273, MUIZENBERG 7950, WESTERN CAPE
TEL: 27 21 788 8235 FAX: 27 21 788 6577 E-MAIL: colona@link.co.za

Sunshine yellow with sparkling white window frames and a grand pillared entrance tower, Colona Castle stands on the warm False Bay coast and is the perfect place from which to explore the beautiful Cape Peninsula. Within easy reach of Cape Town city centre and the airport, this elegant hotel was originally built in 1929 and has been renovated in Tuscan style. It is luxuriously furnished throughout and commands magnificent views of Table Mountain and Sandvlei Lake to the mountain ranges of Boland and the blue waters of the beach-fringed False Bay. The en suite guest rooms are individually designed, with clever personal touches, offering every comfort plus sea, lake and mountain views. Downstairs is the mysterious Moroccan Room and

the lavish Mogul Suite; upstairs, the serene English Suite, with "his and hers" bathrooms, the Saffron Chinese Suite and the verdant Green Room with private balcony. At the 'peak' is the superb Penthouse Suite, the ultimate in comfort for the most discerning visitor. No expense has been spared on decoration. Breakfast can be enjoyed on a shaded terrace or on a balcony overlooking the Bay. Huge open fires and underfloor heating ensure that guests are cosily warm in the cooler winter months. **Directions:** From Cape Town take the M3 and then the M4 south towards False Bay. **Price guide:** Single R750–R1680; double R580; suites R850–R1295 per person sharing. Smoking on terrace and reception rooms only.

TARRAGONA LODGE

CNR DISA RIVER ROAD & VALLEY ROAD, PO BOX 26887, HOUT BAY 7872
TEL: 27 21 790 5080 FAX: 27 21 790 5095 E-MAIL: lodge@tarragona.co.za

Tarragona Lodge stands gleaming white and majestic on the thickly wooded slopes of Table Mountain in the beautiful Hout Bay Valley. It offers outstanding views of the Cape Peninsula ranges and, being just a 20 minutes drive from the hustle and bustle of central Cape Town, is a convenient and ideal venue in which to relax and relieve the stress and strain of daily routine and modern living. Built in Cape European style this elegant guesthouse has everything that visitors could desire. Position, tranquillity, comfort, excellent service, clean, fresh sunshine air. Tension visibly melts away as guests slip into the heated swimming pool or sit back with a cocktail in the mature and colourful landscaped gardens. Nine spacious and bright en suite bedrooms incorporate lounge areas and balconies with commanding valley and mountain views. Each room has all modern facilities from satellite television and international electrical sockets to built-in-safes and tea and coffee making services. A cosy, self-catering Crofter's Cottage in the grounds is also available. There is an extremely comfortable lounge and bar and breakfast is taken in a charming and cool dining room with huge picture window views of the scenic surrounds. Picnic hampers can be made up for guests to enjoy in the garden or to take on sightseeing travels. Some of the Cape's best beaches and golf courses are close by. **Directions:** Take the M63 south from Cape Town. Price guide: Single R415–R490; double/twin R295–R395 per person sharing.

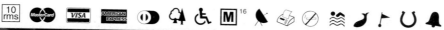

VILLA BELMONTE MANOR HOUSE

33 BELMONT AVENUE, ORANJEZICHT, CAPE TOWN
TEL: 27 21 462 1576 FAX: 27 21 462 1579 E-MAIL: villabel@iafrica.com

Built in 1903 in the Cape Dutch Colonial style, the Villa Belmonte presents the visitor with breathtakingly beautiful views. Embraced by the grandeur of Table Mountain and Table Bay, with the city of Cape Town stretching out towards a blue sea alive with ships and yachts, these are sublime surroundings. Owners Cliff and Tabea Jacobs converted their elegant home into an exclusive boutique hotel and have been awarded a 4 star grading with a Silver classification for service excellence. All 14 air-conditioned rooms are en suite and individually and stylishly decorated, with superb facilities for every comfort. The gracious lounge with its cosy, well-stocked bar is an oasis of peace, and for gourmets, the Villa

Belmonte offers excellent cuisine – both à la carte and table d'hôte – enhanced by some of the Cape's best wines, served in the magnificently restored dining room. The well-equipped board rooms accommodate up to 20 persons; full secretarial services and modern communications technology are available in several languages. A splendid pool sparkles in the garden, and numerous sporting facilities are within easy reach. The Villa is ideally located for visits to all areas of the Cape Peninsula. **Directions:** From the city, travel past Mount Nelson Hotel, turn right into Upper Orange Street, and right into Belmont Avenue. Villa Belmonte is the 2nd property on the left. Price guide: Rooms R990–R1480.

THE CLARENDON

67 KLOOF ROAD, FRESNAYE, PO BOX 224, SEAPOINT, CAPE TOWN
TEL: 27 21 439 3224 FAX: 27 21 434 6855 E-MAIL: info@clarendon.co.za

Conveniently situated in the city's prime seafront suburb, The Clarendon is an ideal venue for all visitors wishing to enjoy the delights of Cape Town. It is a small, elegant, building offering magnificent panoramic mountain and sea views. Beaches, shops and restaurants are within an easy stroll and the popular Victoria and Alfred waterfront is just 5 minutes drive away. The Clarendon Guest House has a very new feel about it. Pastel coloured walls enhance the quality fabrics and discreetly tasteful furnishings throughout the public rooms, which are adorned daily with vases and bowls of fresh cut flowers. The ambience is one of understated luxury. There are seven extremely comfortable and spacious bedrooms, including a

delightful self-catering garden suite which is especially attractive to visitors with children. All the bedrooms are individually decorated, stylish and have good views through tall, wide windows. Guests enjoy all modern facilities, including air conditioning, television and a safe in their room. Full buffet and continental breakfasts are served in the light, airy dining room and dinner is available on request. For relaxation there is a small, private garden with a sparkling swimming pool surrounded by a shady patio on which to lie back and enjoy a cool drink, a good book or a quiet nap. Golf, tennis, riding and fishing can be arranged. **Directions:** The hotel is in central Cape Town. Airport shuttle by arrangement. Price guide: Rooms: R570–R1500.

38

HUIJS HAERLEM

25 MAIN DRIVE, SEAPOINT 8005, CAPE TOWN
TEL: 27 21 434 6434 FAX: 27 21 439 2506 E-MAIL: haerlem@iafrica.com

This small, beautiful, colonial-style guest house is made even more charming by the friendliness and attentiveness of owners Johan and Kees. Nothing is too much trouble for them and they appear to be on hand every minute of the day to serve the needs of guests and offer advice on where to go and what to see on a day's outing. Peace and tranquillity are the keynotes of the whole house. Set high above Sea Point, it is exquisitely furnished throughout with fine Dutch antiques. The five upstairs bedrooms and four new suites in the adjoining house offer all modern requirements, from television, tea and coffee making facilities to underfloor heating and punkah fan. Each room is spacious, en suite, extremely comfortable and tastefully decorated with attention to detail. Some have views over the Atlantic Ocean while guests in other rooms enjoy mountain scenery. Excellent breakfasts are served either on the terrace alongside the solar-heated pool, the sun room or the intimate dining room. The terrace and gardens offer breathtaking views over Robben Island and Bloubergstrand. The waterfront, beaches and city centre with its wide variety of restaurants are nearby. **Directions:** From Airport/City take N2 towards Cape Town, follow sign 'City via Eastern Boulevard'. Follow sign 'City via Strand Street', staying in left lane. Strand Street becomes High Level Road. Cross traffic lights at Glengariff Road. Turn left at Rhine Road and 1st left into Main Drive. Price guide: Rooms R360–R650.

WINCHESTER MANSIONS

221 BEACH ROAD, SEAPOINT, 8005 CAPE TOWN
TEL: 27 21 434 2351 FAX: 27 21 434 0215 E-MAIL: sales@winchester.co.za

Gracious and stylish, Winchester Mansions' atmosphere, courtesy and personal service recalls the more genteel years of the mid 1920s when this hotel was built overlooking Table Bay. Its discreet old world charm has delighted and attracted visitors from far and wide. Recently refurbished, traditional colonial charm blends with all the comforts of a modern, four-star establishment. Marble floors, fine antiques, original art works, delicate room colouring, exquisite drapes and furnishing create a warm, luxurious ambience. The guestrooms have under-carpet heating, ceiling fans, television, telephone, mini-bar and beautiful bathrooms reminiscent of yesteryear. Each bedroom has an original painting by a well-known South African artist and a sea or mountain view. The 18 lavish suites have private lounges with panoramic sea views. Encircled by palm trees and fountains, a wonderfully quiet colonnaded courtyard built in the style of an Italian piazza makes the ideal setting for a romantic dinner under the night stars. The elegant, more formal restaurant fronting the courtyard offers appetising à la carte Cape cuisine. Light meals are also served throughout the day on the terrace overlooking the Atlantic Ocean. Guests can admire magnificent sunsets whilst sipping a cocktail at the Elephant Walk Bar. The beach with its multitude of watersports is opposite the hotel. **Directions:** Seapoint is reached by the Table Bay N1 road. Price guide: Rooms R490–R765; suite R630–R1280.

STEENBERG COUNTRY HOTEL

PO BOX 10802, STEENBERG ESTATE 7945, CONSTANTIA VALLEY, CAPE TOWN
TEL: 27 21 713 2222 FAX: 27 21 713 2221 E-MAIL: hotel@iafrica.com

The hotel buildings date back to 1682 and have been most carefully restored achieving the status of a National Monument. Catherina Ustings was the first owner and she named the original farm 'Swaaneweide', meaning the 'feeding place for Swans' which today is the Steenberg Estate producing some of the country's finest wines. Situated in the serene calm of the Constantia Valley, Steenberg offers a panoramic view over False Bay and the convenience of a private golf course designed by Peter Matkovich and available to hotel guests. The craftsmanship of the interiors transcends time, with wooden ceilings, Yellowwood floors and the original fixtures and fittings that you would expect to find in this important old Cape Dutch homestead dating from the end of the 17th century. The comfort and facilities for contemporary guests match those of the finest accommodation. Each air conditioned en suite room is thoughtfully furnished with antiques and features views across the vineyards and well kept gardens. The restaurant is exceptional and serves Cape Continental dishes and delicacies in a Cape Dutch setting. **Directions**: Take the Tokai/Retreat exit from the M3. Turn right into Tokai road at the stop. Take the left turn at the traffic circle into Steenberg road. Steenberg Estate is on your right. Turn right into Steenberg Estate and follow signs to the hotel. Price guide: Rooms R900–R1500; suite R1600–R2500.

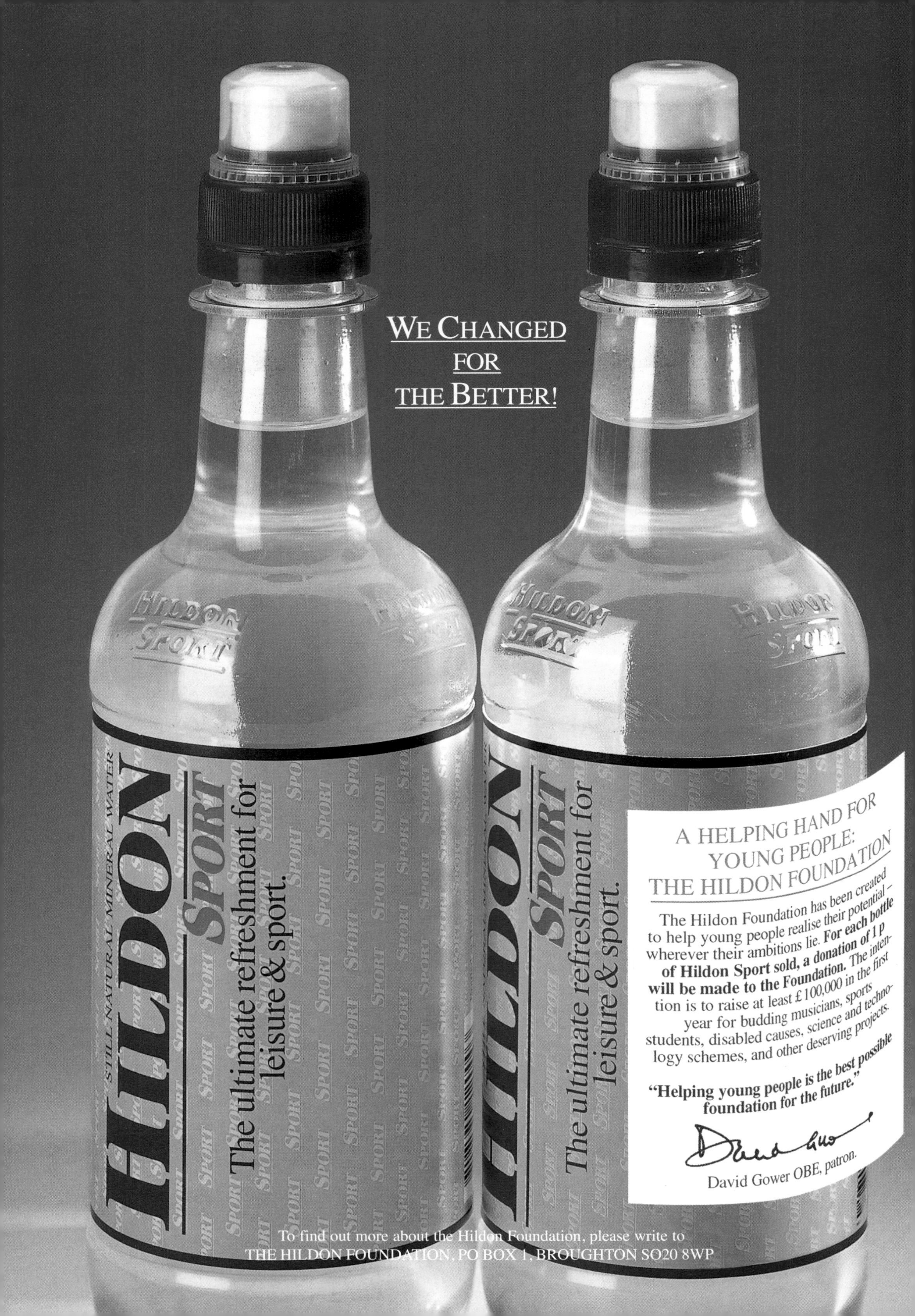

WE CHANGED
FOR
THE BETTER!

STILL NATURAL MINERAL WATER

HILDON SPORT

The ultimate refreshment for leisure & sport.

HILDON SPORT

The ultimate refreshment for leisure & sport.

A HELPING HAND FOR
YOUNG PEOPLE:
THE HILDON FOUNDATION

The Hildon Foundation has been created
to help young people realise their potential –
wherever their ambitions lie. **For each bottle
of Hildon Sport sold, a donation of 1 p
will be made to the Foundation.** The inten-
tion is to raise at least £100,000 in the first
year for budding musicians, sports
students, disabled causes, science and technology schemes, and other deserving projects.

**"Helping young people is the best possible
foundation for the future."**

David Gower OBE, patron.

To find out more about the Hildon Foundation, please write to
THE HILDON FOUNDATION, PO BOX 1, BROUGHTON SO20 8WP

EASTERN CAPE

LESOTHO

KWAZULU-NATAL

FREE STATE

SMITHFIELD

Drakensburg

EASTERN CAPE

PORT SHEPSTONE

NORTHERN CAPE

GARIEP DAM NATURE RESERVE

MACLEAR

MIDDELBURG

STEYNSBURG

ELLIOT

Mkambati Nature Reserve

PORT EDWARD

UMTATA

QUEENSTOWN

GRAAFF-REINET

CRADDOCK

COFFEE BAY

WESTERN CAPE

KAROO

ABERDEEN

KAROO

MOUNTAIN ZEBRA PARK

GONUBIE MOUTH

EAST LONDON

WILLOWMORE

GRAHAMSTOWN

46

ADDO ELEPHANT PARK

UITENHAGE

44

PORT ALFRED

KENTON-ON-SEA

SNAKE PARK

45

PORT ELIZABETH

48 47

JEFFREY'S BAY

PLETTENBERG BAY

St FRANCIS BAY

AUCKLANDS COUNTRY HOUSE

PO BOX 997, GRAHAMSTOWN 6140, EASTERN CAPE
TEL: 27 466 222 401 FAX: 27 466 225 682 E-MAIL: info@aucklands.co.za

This beautifully constructed country house is situated in the heart of the Eastern Cape and holds within its jurisdiction, 272 hectares of prime, unspoiled bush. Through this incredible scenery roams a plethora of animals and birds, mingling and grazing amongst the huge number of enticingly natural and indigenous vegetation. The homestead itself is as stylish as it is accommodating, with huge open plan areas that let all the warmth and beauty of the surroundings flood their way in. The comfortable furniture is neat and elegant and obviously of recent design. Each room is decorated in an individual style, simple yet pleasant colours make them inviting to any guest, whilst all the necessary features are at their disposal. Diners can relax with the host, Ian, over drinks before sampling the cuisine which is nothing less than exquisite and is prepared by the gracious hostess, Cindy. Other pastimes include relaxing over a game of croquet, indulging in a spot of tennis, swimming or exploring the ponds, terraces and gardens, abundant with flora and fauna. Aucklands Country House is a mere one hour's drive away from Addo Elephant Park and other Big Five game reserves. **Directions**: 8km from Grahamstown on N2 towards Port Elizabeth. Price guide: Rooms R440–R640 per person.

HACKLEWOOD HILL COUNTRY HOUSE

152 PROSPECT ROAD, WALMER, PORT ELIZABETH 6070, EASTERN CAPE
TEL: 27 41 5811300 FAX: 27 41 5814155

Built as a Victorian Manor House in 1898, this elegant and stately four star silver hotel stands in the peaceful and exclusive surroundings of the leafy suburbs of Walmer. It is superbly furnished with period pieces, exquisite fabrics and fine paintings. Excellent in every way, Hacklewood Hill exudes comfort and warmth and offers guests unsurpassed luxury in classic country house tradition. Old fashioned ambience, attention and service have been captured perfectly in the Drawing Room with its magnificent fireplace and French doors leading directly to a large pool in the wonderfully colourful English country garden. The spacious, individually decorated bedrooms also offer guests the opportunity to enjoy the beauty of the garden from private balconies or verandahs. The comfort of the eight en suite bedrooms is enhanced by air-conditioning and heating. Full English country breakfasts, light lunches and imaginative dinners are provided by the duo of cordon bleu chefs in the beautifully appointed dining room. The cellar houses an impressive selection of wines and diners can personally select a vintage to complement their meal. There is a tennis court in the garden, golf and a variety of watersports nearby. **Directions:** From N2 (from Cape Town) take 'City' offramp. Turn right into William Moffat Expressway, after approximately 4 km turn left into Main Road; turn right into 10th Avenue, then first right into Prospect Road. Price guide: Rooms from R800 per person sharing.

SHAMWARI GAME RESERVE

PO BOX 32017, SUMMERSTRAND, PORT ELIZABETH 6019
TEL: 27 42 203 1111 FAX: 27 42 235 1224 E-MAIL: shamwaribooking@global.co.za

Stretching along the Bushman's river halfway between Port Elizabeth and Grahamstown lies Shamwari, the Southernmost big game reserve in Africa. Shamwari has been awarded international recognition for its contribution to conservation in harmony with tourism and is Malaria free. Early morning and evening game drives throughout the 18,000 hectare private reserve bring guests close to rhino, elephant, buffalo, hippo, lion, giraffe and eighteen species of antelope. Highly experienced and knowledgeable game rangers accompany each game drive helping to enrich guests experience of the history of settlers in the area, the diversity of plant life, animal species and birdlife all in natural abundance. A choice of accommodation is represented by Long Lee Manor, an Edwardian mansion with adjacent garden suite enjoying sweeping views of the valley towards the Bushmans river. Lobengula Lodge offers a presidential suite and de luxe double bedrooms for a 'five star' African experience. Three Settler Lodges built around 1860, Carn Ingly, Highfield and Bushmans River Lodge are situated in the heart of the reserve, and each with its own game ranger and chef. Traditional African cooking with a European flavour can be appreciated in the dining room or around the fireside 'lapa'. Gourmet barbecue meals are also prepared. **Directions:** Shamwari can be reached by road (N2) from Port Elizabeth for 65kms towards Grahamstown. Price guide: Rooms R1350–R3300 p.p. fully inclusive.

THE BEACH HOUSE

4 FRANK ROAD, ST FRANCIS BAY 6312, EASTERN CAPE
TEL: 27 42 294 0551/294 1225 FAX: 27 42 294 0748 E-MAIL: info@stfrancisbay.co.za

Owned by Petrea and Lionel Donnelly, who are also hosts at Sandals just a one minute walk, away, the cool and attractive Beach House is the Bay's newest boutique hotel. Opened in December 1999 it is of traditional, thatched Indonesian style and was built, furnished and fitted to cater for a guest's every requirement. Standards, service, privacy and security are high. Situated in the heart of St Francis within a short walk of excellent shops and restaurants it is a guest house that is superb in every way. There is a choice of four luxurious en suite bedrooms, each beautifully and individually decorated and furnished and complete with extra length bed and full modern facilities. All offer spectacular panoramic ocean and bay views. Guests can relax on their own private patios or on the lush green lawns of the tropical gardens overlooking the sea. Beach House has two pools, one nestling among enormous indigenous rocks and the other spilling over into the sea. There are lovely low tide walks along three kilometres of wide open white sandy beach on the one side and a nature-inspired trail along the picturesque rocky peninsula to the quaint harbour on the other. A full range of water sports is available, there is golf, tennis and riding nearby and game reservation excursions can be arranged. **Directions:** N2 towards Port Elizabeth and turn off to Humausdorp. Price guide: Rooms R695–R895 per person.

SANDALS BEACH HOUSE

4 NAPIER ROAD, ST FRANCIS BAY 6312, EASTERN CAPE
TEL: 27 42 294 1225/0551 FAX: 27 42 294 0748 E-MAIL: info@stfrancisbay.co.za

St Francis Bay, with its four kilometre stretch of unspoilt beach, picturesque little harbour and attractive village of traditional thatched houses is situated a comfortable one hour drive from Port Elizabeth. It has everything to make a holiday enjoyable and memorable: mild year-round temperatures, the longest sunshine hours on the South African coast, a malaria-free environment and a host of active sports activities. The unique treed and palm fringed Sandals Beach House stands amongst large ingenuous rocks just 80 metres from the main beach. Decorated in tropical style it offers comfort, elegance and uniqueness and caters for every need of the discerning guest. There is the choice of 10 large, individually decorated luxury bedrooms with private patios and decks. Each is en suite with bath and shower, comfortably furnished down to an extra length bed and with every comfort including satellite television, telephone, hairdryer, coffee and tea making facilities. There is a tastefully decorated, ultra modern dining room with central fireplace in which to relax over a drink at the bar. Hearty breakfasts and excellently prepared and served dinners are enjoyed in the circular dining room or on the cool, undercover pool deck. **Directions:** Take N2 from Cape Town towards Port Elizabeth and turn off to Humausdorp; approximately 18kms to St Francis Bay. Price guide: Rooms R295–R395 per person.

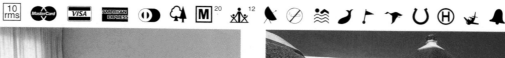

GAUTENG

NORTHERN PROVINCE

MPUMALANGA

NORTHWEST PROVINCE

•MABOPANE

PRETORIA

Voortrekker Monument

Magaliesberg Mountains

HEKPOORT

IRENE
•DOORNKLOOF

Financial District

Caves

KRUGERSDORP

KEMPTON PARK

50

JOHANNESBURG

MPUMALANGA

SOWETO

CARLETONVILLE

ZOO

NIGEL

HEIDELBERG

SEBOKENG

SHARPEVILLE •VEREENIGING

MPUMALANGA

FREE STATE

VAAL DAM

SAXON

36 SAXON ROAD, SANDHURST 2132, GAUTENG
TEL: 27 11 292 6000 FAX: 27 11 292 6001 E-MAIL: reservations@saxon.co.za

This stylish and serene hotel is where Nelson Mandela relaxed to edit his autobiography 'Long Walk to Freedom' following release from imprisonment. Saxon nestles in the exclusive Sandhurst suburb of Sandton and boasts ethnic African elegance combined with personalised attention to detail. Surrounded by six acres of landscaped gardens the hotel embraces a natural environment where the central point is a magnificent 920 sq metre swimming pool. Above the pool is a terrace overlooking the indigenous gardens with the city as a backdrop. Behind the hotel's slate-grey façade visitors will be immediately impressed by the modernistic reception area featuring twin staircases sweeping around a glass dome from which natural light enhances the contemporary native décor and handcrafted ethnic art. 28 suites of various sizes have large bay windows overlooking the gardens or pool. Each beautifully decorated and furnished suite has every facility, from large screen TV and high tech sound systems to a workstation fitted with multi telephone, fax and ISDN lines. World class chefs ensures excellent cuisine in the superb dining room. An attractive cocktail bar leads off the expansive pool terrace and there is a fully equipped health centre with gym, beauty salon and steam rooms. **Directions:** From N1 North take Jan Smuts exit to William Nichol. Price guide: Suite R3900.

KWAZULU~NATAL

MPUMALANGA

SWAZILAND

FREE STATE

UTRECHT

BLOEDRIVER

Ndumo Game Reserve

59

Tembe Elephant Park

Kosi Bay Nature Reserve

60

61

Mkuzi Game Reserve

58

55 **65**

63

57

St. Lucia Estuary

64 **52**

Dingaan's Kraal

LADYSMITH

Mont-aux-Sources

Fort Durnford Museum

ESTCOURT

ESHOWE

RICHARDS BAY

Valley of 1000 Hills

Drakensberg Mountains

Royal Natal National

53 **62** **54**

PIETERMARITZBURG

UMHLANGA ROCKS

DURBAN

Natal Lion Park

EASTERN CAPE

56

IXOPO

MARGATE

PORT EDWARD

ISANDLWANA LODGE

PO BOX 30, ISANDLWANA, KWAZULU –NATAL 3005
TEL: +27 34 271 8301 FAX: +27 34 271 8306 E-MAIL: isand@icon.co.za

This is a wild, beautiful landscape where, long ago, spear-wielding warriors clashed with British redcoat invaders armed with rifles. History now, but still enthralling to today's visitors seeking to soak up timeless atmosphere on a holiday with a difference. Isandlwana Lodge is in the heart of Zululand, nestling among majestic hills overlooking Mount Isandlwana. It was in January 1879 that a column of redcoats under the command of General Lord Chelmsford was wiped out by King Cetshwayo's Zulu army, who then was repulsed at the barricaded post at Rorke's Drift, just a 25 minutes drive from the Lodge. Isandlwana's luxurious accommodation is carved in the iNyoni Rock formations on top of which the Zulu commander stood to direct the battle. 12 en suite rooms offer every facility for a memorable stay. Décor is cool and tasteful and the furniture a comfortable mixture of traditional and modern. From bedroom balconies and public rooms there are unparalleled views from crisp dawn light to splendid African sunsets. Panoramic windows stretch the length of the dining room where excellent cuisine is served. Guests can cool off in the lodge's rock pool, trek around the countryside or enjoy one of many battlefield tours led by historian Rob Gerrard, FRGS, some of which can be offered on horseback. **Directions:** From Johannesburg drive via Newcastle to Dundee; take A68 towards Babanango. Price guide (half board): Single R720–R990; double/twin R630–R800 per person.

www.isandlwana.co.za

ORCHID VALLEY

PO BOX 123, UNDERBERG 3257, KWAZULU-NATAL
TEL: 27 33 701 1700 FAX: 27 33 701 1465 E-MAIL: hosie@futurenet.co.za

Grassland sloping down to the river valley and then rising upwards frame the unspoilt Southern Drakensberg landscape. In winter, peaks to the west stand gleaming white snow capped; in summer the dark green mountain slopes are splashed with swathes of red and orange wildflower colours. These are the fabulous views guests see and absorb from the manicured lawned garden, lounge and bar of this peaceful Lodge retreat, a comfortable 2 hours' drive west from Durban. The elusive bearded vulture flies overhead, herds of eland 'tip-toe' through from the western boundary National Park. Orchid Valley has over 3.5km of private river frontage and a tumbling waterfall just a short walk from the Lodge. Otters and giant kingfishers can be spotted and a dip in the natural pools followed by breakfast or sundowners offer guests a memorable experience far from the bustling outside world. Four comfortably appointed double bedrooms with en suite bathrooms and every modern facility cater for the discerning guest. Chef Olivia Hosie, who has served five-course meals from locations as diverse as the Botswana Chobe desert to the 5 star Table Bay Hotel in Cape Town, produces superb cuisine in the dining room, complemented by an extensive list of fine wines. **Directions:** Underberg, approximately 1 h drive west of the Johannesburg-Durban highway. Price guide (all-inclusive): Double/twin: R684 per person sharing.

OLD HALLIWELL COUNTRY INN

PO BOX 201, HOWICK 3290, KWAZULU-NATAL
TEL: 27 33 330 2602 FAX: 27 33 330 3430 E-MAIL: haliwell@mweb.co.za

Steeped in history, this original stone house dates back to the 1830's and was sited overlooking the Karkloof Valley on the wagon route to the "interior". Today, this fine old country inn offers guests the most civilised amenities. A relaxing informality, roaring log fires, comfortable sofas, the sparkle of silver, fresh flowers and convivial company conspire to work their magic on the weary traveller. The old stables that surround the sloping lawns accommodate spacious bedrooms offering every essential comfort, from private verandas to the welcome of your own log fire. Guests gather in Steven's Bar after a day at leisure in the beautiful Natal Midlands where spectacular waterfalls, exquisite wild flowers and an extraordinary variety of birds delight the mind and eye. The more adventurous can enjoy visiting the majestic Drakensberg via the breathtaking Sani Pass or horse riding, golf and trout fishing on a dam nearby. The dining room has fine menus featuring European and regional dishes capitalising on fresh local produce including Drakensberg Trout! **Directions:** Old Halliwell is only a four hour drive from Johannesburg or one hour from Durban. From the N3 take exit 114 to Currys Post/Lions River. Straight up the hill and left at the 'T' Junction. Price guide: Rooms R450–R600.

FALAZA GAME PARK

PO BOX 13, HLUHLUWE 3960, KWAZULU-NATAL
TEL: 27 35 562 0319 FAX: 27 35 562 0739 E-MAIL: resfalaz@mweb.co.za

With an abundance of wildlife and lush, green land, this privately owned game park overlooks the shoreline and reefs of St Lucia's world heritage site False Bay and protects the remnants of a once mighty sand forest which evolved over 150,000 years ago. Antelope, waterbuck, the rare suni, zebra, giraffe, hyena, leopard, hippo and rhino can be spotted by guests as they game view on foot, horseback or in four-wheel drive vehicles. Falaza is named after a veteran of King Cetshwaya's Zulu Impi who, over a century ago, fought against British forces at the battle of Isandhlwana. Tented en suite accommodation with tiled floors, modern comforts and wooden sun decks are scattered among tall trees and dense vegetation which affords privacy and seclusion. Excellent cuisine and wines are enjoyed either under the stars in a boma, in the spacious and attractive thatched roof dining room or in the openness of a fully equipped conference lapa. Each has its own bar and attentive, personal service. A boat trip along the waterways of Falaza's Wilderness Park is an unforgettable experience, with the cruise boat comfortably carrying up to 20. Falaza is ideal for visiting South Africa's major game reserves, and the authentic Dumazulu village is one of many local attractions. **Directions:** From Durban take N2 to Hluhluwe, follow signs to Falsebay and then turn right at False Bay Gate. Falaza is 1.7kms on your right. Price guide: Single R565–R920; double R525–R760 per person.

LYTHWOOD LODGE

PO BOX 17, LIDGETTON 3270, KWAZULU-NATAL
TEL: 27 33 234 4666 FAX: 27 33 234 4668 E-MAIL: info@lythwood.co.za

The long gravel road climbing gently to Lythwood Lodge simply adds to the anticipation of something rather special. The journey is well worth the delightful surprise upon arrival. Built in 1940 by Italian prisoners of war, using local stone, Lythwood overlooks sloping lawns with acres of indigenous forest climbing the mountains behind, this is a truly gracious hotel in a beautiful setting. The bedrooms and bathrooms are both stylish and spacious and of course the ballroom has a sprung floor! The attention to detail is inspiring, from handmade Swaziland drinking glasses in the bar, to the carefully tended herbs in the vegetable garden, everything is carefully considered and nothing left to chance. The accommodation is luxurious with acres of mahogany, antiques and white linen. Dining guests at Lythwood may submit to the deft creativity of Kathy Adams, the Chef. Her choice of dishes rewards the most critical palate and as a treat for breakfast you may if you wish have Scottish Kippers! This is walking country, for bird watching, visiting the art and craft centres nearby or trout fishing. **Directions**: Lythwood is 24km from the Howick/Midmar exit N3 or 35 km from Nottingham Road exit N3. Price guide: Rooms R1074–R1343.

MAKAKATANA BAY LODGE

PO BOX 65, MTUBATUBA, KWAZULU-NATAL 3935
TEL: 27 35 550 4189 FAX: 27 35 550 4198 E-MAIL: info@makakatana.co.za

Exclusively situated in the proclaimed Greater St Lucia Wetland Park Reserve, the largest marine lake in Africa, Makakatana remains the only privately owned lodge set within this pristine World Heritage Site. The land has been owned by the Morrison family since the 1930s, and the glorious, unspoilt wetland provides an undeniable attraction to lovers of wildlife. Hugh and Leigh-Ann have created an intimate luxury lodge and welcome guests to their stylishly decorated home from home. Private air-conditioned suites are splashed with a mixture of Eastern and African interior styles. Enjoy a relaxing holiday or indulge in the wildlife, wetland and beach splendours. Lake St Lucia is home to 367 bird species one of

only a few places in Africa that support such a concentration of bird life. Experience the captivating wetlands by boat and seek out hippo and crocodile. The virtually untouched beaches and pristine waters have the only turtle breeding grounds and tropical coral reefs in the sub-continent. Plan a day trip to see the big five in the nearby world-famous Hluhluwe/Umfolozi Game Reserve. **Directions:** The lodge is a 2½ hour drive from Durban (1 hour from Richards Bay) along N2, turning right 25 km after Mtubatuba Road, taking 'Charters Creek/Fanies Island' turnoff. Follow road for 14 km, take right fork on dirt track, and continue for another 3km. Price guide (full board): Rooms R1200–R1600 per person.

MKUZE FALLS GAME LODGE

PO BOX 248, PONGOLA 3170, KWAZULU-NATAL
TEL: 27 34 414 1018 FAX: 27 34 414 1021 E-MAIL: mkuze@mweb.co.za

With a beautiful mountain backdrop, this reserve lodge on the northern bank of the Mkuze River overlooks a spectacular waterfall and the river. It offers an authentic taste of African bush in the heart of one of the country's most diverse conservation areas and is host to a diversity of flora and fauna. Elephant, white and black rhino, buffalo, leopard, hippo, crocodile and numerous antelope species roam the 6,200 hectares. Guests can see them at first hand on walking or open vehicle safaris led by experienced rangers and trackers. At 'base' there are nine luxurious, air-conditioned thatched chalets which can accommodate 18 guests in style and comfort. Each chalet has a private deck with views of Shembe mountain. En suite facilities include a plunge pool and outside shower which are shielded from adjacent accommodation by thick indigenous vegetation. Guests can meet up and enjoy a drink in the central lodge's delightful lounge, bar and dining area. A traditional outdoor reeded enclosure, known as a 'boma', is the venue for delectable evening meals around an open fire, where Zulu dancing and entertainment is a feature. Raised wooden decks surround a swimming pool from which to enjoy river and waterfall views. The lodge is close to the southern border of Swaziland and an ideal stopover for travellers between Kruger National Park and Durban. **Directions:** Leave N2 at Pongola and take R66 towards Nongoma. Price guide: Chalet R1,000–1,600; suite R1,200–R2,060.

NDUMO WILDERNESS CAMP

PO BOX 78573, SANDTON 2146
TEL: 27 11 883 0747 FAX: 27 11 883 0911

This camp is very close to nature; a remote place offering visitors a truly wonderful opportunity to observe wildlife at its best. Ndumo Wilderness Camp is situated on the edge of the Banzi Pan within the Ndumo Game Reserve, just south of the Mozambique border. It is one of the oldest reserves in South Africa, having been proclaimed in 1924, and boasts approximately 60% of all bird species found in South Africa. Game includes both black and white rhino, buffalo, giraffe, blue wildebeest, zebra, hippo, crocodile, antelope, nyala, red duiker and the elusive suni. The camp offers eight spacious tented rooms with en suite bathrooms and there is a separate bar, lounge and dining room under thatch. The entire camp is raised up on a wooden deck and linked with a walkway several metres above the ground. All tents are comfortably furnished, safari style, and equipped with everything from a torch and laundry bag to a mosquito coil, insect repellent spray and a birdlist. The surrounding area is magnificent and time at Ndumo is mostly spent on exploratory walks through forests of fig trees and through the bush or driving in open 4x4 vehicles around the various pans. Local villagers are employed in the camp and provide excellent service. **Directions:** From Durban, take N2 north to Mkuze. About 10km beyond Mkuze turn right signposted Josini, Ndumo and Sodwana Bay. Price guide (incl. all meals): Rooms R995 per person sharing.

SHAYAMOYA GAME LODGE

PO BOX 784, PONGOLA 3170
TEL: 27 34 435 1110 FAX: 27 34 435 1008 E-MAIL: shayalodge@saol.com

Relax and listen to the mystical sounds of Africa from your luxurious thatched chalet and take in the panoramic view of Pongolapoort Lake, Lebombo Mountains and Pongola Nature Reserve from your own viewing deck. Situated on a ridge bordering the reserve, Shayamoya is the perfect place to unwind and be at one with nature. For the keen angler, Shayamoya specialises in the challenging sport of tiger fishing. The lake is the only destination in South Africa where this freshwater game fish is found. Activities are plentiful from game viewing by vehicle or boat, golf, canoe, guided walks and elephant tracking, to a cooling dip in the pool. The Lodge is the perfect venue for small conferences and team building gatherings. Indulge in some South African cuisine or enjoy a traditional braai under the African sky. Your hosts, Brian and Denise Blevin, provide a friendly and welcoming service and see that you have everything possible to make your stay a memorable and happy experience. The lodge is also ideally located to break the long journey from Kruger Park or Johannesburg to Maputaland/Kwazulu-Natal. **Directions:** Between the towns of Mkuze and Pongola, take the road from the N2 to Golela/Swaziland border post. 2km up a hill and turn left at the Shayamoya gate. 1km on dirt road to reception. Price guide: Rooms R670–R885 per person including game drives, boat cruises and all meals.

WHITE ELEPHANT LODGE

PO BOX 792, PONGOLA 3170, KWAZULU-NATAL
RESERVATIONS TEL: 27 86 110 0517 LODGE TEL: 27 34 435 1117 FAX: 27 34 435 1117 E-MAIL: info@whiteelephantlodge.co.za

The history and romance of a bygone era are truly captured at this unique East African safari concept. Originally built in the 1920s, the 16-bed White Elephant Lodge offers a secluded retreat in the heart of unspoilt savannah bushveld. Surrounded by the imposing Lebombo Mountains and shimmering waters of Lake Jozini, its eight luxurious tented chalets are fitted with magnificent Victorian style bathrooms which open onto the bush, outdoor canvas shower enclosures, private verandahs, and a personal bar. Excellent cuisine and a personalised service contribute further towards the relaxed ambience of this intimate yet awe-inspiring experience. The lake provides many attractions, from spectacular Tiger fishing to early morning game viewing cruises and late afternoon sunset excursions. Pongola Game Reserve, the second oldest in the world, acts as sanctuary to a huge range of wildlife, including giraffe, wildebeest, zebra, rhino, impala and leopard. The Reserve is a co-operative conservation project between private landowners, tribal communities and Government Conservation Services, so guests can take the unique opportunity of participating in an elephant monitoring programme. Visits to many other nearby Zululand game and nature reserves can be organised upon request. **Directions:** Take N2 between the villages of Pongola and Mkuze. Main gate entrance at sign 'Pongola Game Reserve'. Price guide: Single R1100–R1370; double/twin R780–R970 per person.

HARTFORD HOUSE

PO BOX 31, MOOI RIVER 3300, KWAZULU-NATAL
TEL: 27 33 2632713 FAX: 27 33 2632818 E-MAIL: info@hartford.co.za

For rather more than a century the Hartford and Summerhill Farms have been inextricably linked. Royalty and great Ministers of State have trodden this beautiful property within sight of Giant's Castle in the foothills of the Drakensberg Mountains. In 1991 the internationally renowned Summerhill Stud acquired the historic Hartford Country Lodge and restored it tastefully, brick by brick, to its former Victorian glory. Today, Hartford House languishes amidst manicured gardens abundant with cherry trees and roses, surrounded by sun dappled valleys at the heart of Thoroughbred and champion stock country. Dining on the verandah is a magical experience amidst candles and the delights of exquisite regional dishes and fine wines. This truly is the home of good conversation, old whiskies and classic horses. The suites are magnificently appointed and imaginatively decorated with ingenious touches of creativity. They are the essence of comfort, with fireplaces and underfloor heating for cooler nights. Hartford House is renowned for its Stud Farm tours, the Stallions of the Sheikhs of Dubai, the Zulu and Anglo-Boer War Battlefields, the Midlands Meander, nearby game viewing and the Drakensberg Mountains. **Directions:** 90 minutes from Durban, exit the N3 Mooi River/Treverton Interchange and follow signs. Price guide: Rooms R330–R645.

PAKAMISA PARADISE

PO BOX 1097, PONGOLA, KWAZULU-NATAL 3170
TEL: +27 34 413 3559 FAX: +27 34 413 1817 E-MAIL: pakamisa@pga.dorea.co.za

The vast Pondoro Game Reserve offers an unparalleled bush experience and teems with a variety of wildlife. At its heart is the very exclusive Pakamisa Paradise Hotel, whose beautiful colonial Italo-Spanish architecture blends superbly with the raw natural beauty of its surrounds. Owner Isabella von Stepski manages the estate with style and courtesy, providing gracious living and ultimate luxury for 16 VIP guests in eight chalets, each with double bedroom, deluxe bathroom, lounge, veranda and every comfort. The El Prado restaurant offers an experience in fine dining within a stylish atmosphere, from delicious breakfasts and lunches to 5-o'clock teas and Gala Dinners with concert entertainment. Guests can enjoy drinks at a bar beside the rock pool or in the intimate Hunter's Bar. In the evenings, sundowners are served around an open campfire. Horse lovers will be impressed by the magnificent Arabian horses and can take riding lessons or explore the unspoilt wilderness from horseback. Clay pigeon shooting, photo safaris and birdwatching can be organised, as well as guided bush walks with picnic breaks. German, French, Spanish and Portuguese spoken. **Directions:** Via air-shuttle from Johannesburg to Pongola. Price guide: Double R1500-R2200.

ISIBINDI ZULU LODGE

PO BOX 1593, ESHOWE 3815
TEL: +27 35 474 1504 FAX: +27 35 474 1490 E-MAIL: isibindi@iafrica.com

Isibindi Zulu Lodge rises majestically from the rugged bushveld of the old Zulu kingdom and offers guests an unsurpassed battlefields cultural and game experience. Owner Brett Gehren provides excellent hospitality at his tranquil lodge which was inspired by traditional Zulu architecture. Six beehive style suites, equipped with every modern facility, afford magnificent views over the Isibindi Eco-Reserve and Zululand. This 4000 acre private game reserve is situated approximately 5km from the internationally acclaimed battlefield of Rorke's Drift and Isandlwana and has habitats ranging from grassland and valley bushlands to riverine forests. Game and birdlife is abundant. The Lodge's resident historian, Prince Sibudso Shibe, whose great-grandfather fought in the battle of Isandlwana, leads guests on tours of the battlefields and regales evening diners with stories of the tragedy of these heroic battles. Guests can also visit a local Zulu village, join a family for a traditional meal and enjoy Zulu dancing. After a day spotting wildlife from a Land Rover or whitewater rafting on the Buffalo river, imaginative meals created by the talented chef may be savoured. **Directions:** From Jo'burg drive via Newcastle to Dundee. Then take R33 towards Greytown, after 14km turn left at Rorke's Drift sign. Go through Rorke's Drift and follow signs. From Durban, take N3 to Pietermaritzburg, then R33 from Greytown to Dundee. Price guide (all incl.): Single R925–R1020; double/twin R715–R785.

NIBELLA LAKE LODGE

PO BOX 10305, MARINE PARADE, KWAZULU-NATAL 4056
TEL: 27 31 337 4222 FAX: 27 31 368 2322 E-MAIL: nibela@goodersons.co.za

This is Africa at its most glorious. An exclusive, remote lodge nestling at the tip of the Nibela Peninsula, surrounded by previously inaccessible woodlands and overlooking magnificent Lake St Lucia, the country's largest body of natural body. The lake forms part of the Greater St Lucia Wetland Park. It is 60kms long, and an estimated 1,200 crocodiles and 800 hippo live in its shallow waters. There are fish eagles, flamingos, pelican and giant heron, and sharks have been spotted. Nibela Lake Lodge is unobtrusive, blends into the forest surrounds and is reached only by a 20 minutes boat ride over these waters. Eleven luxurious, thatched lodges stand high up in the coolness of a canopy of trees, offering solitude and tranquillity. Each lodge has exquisitely decorated rooms which include an en suite bathroom with shower and a restful lounge area. This leads onto a wide wooden deck from where spectacular forest and waterway views can be enjoyed. A restaurant seating up to 30 specialises in excellent cuisine and personalised service. There's a relaxing lounge opening onto a wraparound wooden deck, a cosy and popular bar and a swimming pool. Organised game, bird, forest and shoreline walks are available, together with morning or sundowner croc and hippo spotting cruises. **Directions:** A 280kms drive from Durban to False Bay Park. Price guide (fully inclusive): Single R1295; double R995 per person sharing.

PREFERRED PARTNERS

Preferred partners are those organisations specifically chosen and exclusively recommended by Johansens for the quality and excellence of their products and services for the mutual benefit of Johansens recommendations, readers and independent travellers. For further details, please contact Fiona Patrick at Johansens on 0207 566 9700.

MPUMALANGA

NORTHERN PROVINCE

DRAKENSBERG

PILGRIM'S REST

Sabie

KRUGER NATIONAL PARK

MOZAMBIQUE

68
69
70 72
71

Coal

Loskop Dam Nature Reserve

MIDDELBURG

WITBANK

NELSPRUIT

BARBERTON

GAUTENG

ERMELO

SWAZILAND

Vaal Dam Nature Reserve

STANDERTON

PIET RETIEF

FREE STATE

VOLKSRUST

KWAZULU-NATAL

Casa Do Sol

PO BOX 57, HAZYVIEW 1242, MPUMALANGA
TEL: 27 13 737 8111 FAX: 27 13 737 8166 E-MAIL: casado@soft.co.za

Situated in a 500 hectare nature reserve with giraffe, zebra, a variety of antelope, crocodiles and prolific birdlife, Casa do Sol is an oasis of tranquil pools, shaded glades, streams, peaceful flower gardens and luxurious accommodation encircled by glorious Mpumalanga and within easy reach of Blyde River Canyon and Kruger National Park. Created and run by Wellesley Bailey and his family, the complex consists of attractive casas and villas on either side of cobbled streets. Suites surround a picturesque green where the restaurant and cosy bar create a village atmosphere. The two-storey, double-bedroom executive suite has a large sitting room opening onto a patio with Jacuzzi, sauna and private pool in an enclosed garden. All bedrooms are en suite and have air conditioning, satellite TV and every modern facility. Two pools are surrounded by award-winning tropical gardens of serene beauty. Service is friendly and attentive, and the cuisine, imaginative and sophisticated. Vegetables, fruit and dairy produce are farm-grown, and only the best and freshest are used. Casa do Sol is the ideal base from which to tour the heart of the Lowveld and Kruger National Park or guests can enjoy helicopter picnics, night safaris or individually tailored tours. **Directions:** From Jo'burg take N1 towards Pretoria, N4 to Witbank and Nelspruit, R40 to White River and Hazyview R536 to Casa do Sol. Price guide: Single R440–R660; double R350–R530; suites R500–R2200 per person (all inclusive).

IDUBE GAME RESERVE

RESERVATIONS, PO BOX 2617, NORTHCLIFF 2115
TEL: 27 11 888 3713 FAX: 27 11 888 2181 E-MAIL: iduberes@global.co.za

Situated at the heart of the exclusive Sabi Sand Game Reserve, the Idube Private Game Reserve is a simply designed lodge dedicated to the concept of a genuine bush experience. Elephants, impala and waterbuck roam freely through the beautiful wild gardens, with the reserve comprising a collection of traditional chalets, each with en suite bathrooms, air-conditioning and imperial overhead fans. Run by enthusiasts, the Idube Private Game Reserve serves traditional African dishes in the convivial setting of the boma, where guests can bask in the glow of a log fire. During the afternoon guests can take advantage of the glistening boulder pool, or just relax in the sumptuous gardens.

Within the confines of the Idube Private Game Reserve elephants, rhinos, buffaloes and lions can be found, where visitors regularly catch glimpses of cheetah and wild dogs. Idube's staff have an unequalled knowledge of the surrounding bush, making the lodge's night drives a once in a lifetime experience. The Idube Reserve is also a birdlover's oasis. As many as 300 species inhabit the area, providing ample sustenance for budding ornithologists. Idube is a short drive from the Kruger National Park. **Directions:** From Hazyview, follow the R536 for 34 km, until a fork in the road. Take the lefthand fork, and follow the signs to Idube. Price guide: Rooms R2000 per person sharing per night.

LEOPARD HILLS PRIVATE GAME RESERVE

PO BOX 612, HAZYVIEW 1242, MPUMALANGA
TEL: 27 13 737 6626/7 FAX: 27 13 737 6628 E-MAIL: leopardh@mweb.co.za

Located in the western sector of the Sabi Sand Game Reserve, which flanks Kruger National Park, Leopard Hills is a private game reserve where privacy and excellence of service are guaranteed. The property is a hideaway beyond compare and visitors are stunned by the number of wild animals that pass within view. Composed of eight luxurious suites, each with its own plunge pool commanding unforgettable views of the bush, the lodge promises complete privacy in a truly magical setting. The cuisine and cellar are both exceptional and meals are served at a single table overlooking the bush below. Early in the morning and at night, the lodge offers guests safari drives through the 10,000 hectares of rugged bush that Leopard Hills occupies. The variety of wildlife on show is breathtaking, and visitors can see the whole spectrum of Africa's big game, from lions, elephants and hyenas to cheetah, buffalo and rhino. Guests can also take supervised games walks through the bush. **Directions:** From Johannesburg, take the N12 or N4 to Nelspruit. At White River, take the R40 to Hazyview, turning right onto the R536 in the direction of Paul Kruger Gate. After 34km turn left towards Newington Gate and follow the signs. Price guide: Rooms R3595–R4495 per person.

ULUSABA PRIVATE GAME RESERVE

P.O. BOX 71, SKUKUZA 1350, SABI SAND, MPUMALANGA
TEL: 27 13 735 5460 FAX: 27 13 735 5171 E-MAIL: rock@ulusaba.com

Tennis courts in the bush are the first indication that this lodge is far from ordinary. A steep track takes you up to the 'Kopje' past wonderfully carved figures to Ulusaba Rock Lodge, almost 650 feet above the Lowveld. To be handed a glass of champagne upon arrival and then to realise that the world is literally at your feet, is a heady experience. Dining on Pan-African dishes, influenced by many African cultures, surrounded by the surreal Baroque decoration of the main house is quite magical. Bedrooms are boldy decorated to reflect the culture of the region with viewing decks, full air conditioning and complimentary laundry service. A fully equipped gym, mountain top swimming pool and beauty therapy room and of course superb game drives are just some of the facilities. Children are welcome. Nearby, Ulusaba Safari Lodge, a 'Hemingway' styled timber stilted camp with robust rope (steel) swing bridges connecting the bedrooms and main lodge over a dry river bed teeming with wildlife, offers a truly unique experience. **Directions:** Ulusaba can be reached by air from Skukuza, Nelspruit or Hoedspruit. Private charter can be arranged from Johannesburg to the nearby airstrip. Price guide: Rooms R2,450–10,000.

SAVANNA PRIVATE GAME RESERVE

PO BOX 3619, WHITE RIVER 1240, MPUMALANGA
TEL: 27 13 737 7902 FAX: 27 13 737 7919 E-MAIL: ecologics@soft.co.za

A unique marriage of earthy camp living with the sophistication and luxury of a five-star hotel, the Savanna Private Game Reserve is a unique bush hideaway that guarantees privacy and friendly South African service. Set on a 10,000 hectare swathe of imposing bush situated on the Sabi Sand Game Reserve, the lodge offers visitors unparalleled access to the wildlife of this rugged prelapsarian paradise. The open-air game drives, conducted by rangers and trackers steeped in the culture of the region, are most exhilarating. Aside for the 450 bird species that inhabit the area, visitors also gain intimate access to lions, elephants, buffalo, rhino, cheetah and crocodiles. For those with an interest in indigenous culture, the lodge also offers excursions to nearby Shangaan village where lessons in traditional tribal life may be learnt. The accommodation is nothing short of exceptional, with many of the secluded suites benefiting from their own private swimming pools. The hearty breakfasts are served on an open-air verandah, while dinner is taken either in the starlit boma, or in the South Africa Railway Dining Carriage, dating from the 1914. **Directions:** From Johannesburg, take the N12 or N4 towards Nelspruit. At White River take the R40 to Hazyview, turning right onto R536. After 34 km, just after the Saringwa River follow the signs on the left hand side of the road. Price guide: Rooms R1695–R2995.

NORTHERN PROVINCE

BOTSWANA

ZIMBABWE

MESSINA

SOUTHPANSBERG

THOHOYANDOU

PAFURI

LOUIS TRICHARDT

BOTSWANA

KRUGER

NATIONAL

PARK

ELLISRAS

Coal

Mokolosi
Bird Sanctuary

MOZAMBIQUE

Waterberg

PIETERSBURG/

PERCY FYFE

NATURE

RESERVE

POLOKWANE

77

Makapans
Cave

Makensberg

76

74

WARMBAD

Warm Baths

75

SUN CITY

NORTH-WEST

PROVINCE.

GAUTENG

MPUMALANGA

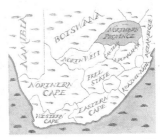

73

TSHUKUDU GAME LODGE

PO BOX 289, HOEDSPRUIT 1380
TEL: 27 15 793 2476 FAX: 27 15 793 2078 E-MAIL: tshukudu@iafrica.com

Tshukudu has been run by Lolly and Ala Sussens as a family operation for 20 years and it has earned the reputation of being one of the most comfortable game lodges in Africa. It is situated in the malaria-free Northern Province which runs close to the famous Kruger National Park, approximately midway between its Northern and Southern boundaries. The Sussens are internationally renowned for their projects to introduce orphaned animals back into the bush and many of these animals, including lion cubs and baby elephants, wander around the lodge and its 5,000 hectares reserve. It is a unique experience for visitors who have never seen wild animals within touching distance. Accommodation is in thatched chalets and rondawels. Each is pleasantly furnished and includes en suite bathrooms with showers. The rooms also have a verandah where guests can relax in cane chairs and sofas and spot the teeming wildlife on the lowveld plains. Ala is renowned for her excellent African cuisine and dining is a delight. The daily room rate is inclusive of three excellent meals, two game drives in open Land Rovers, a morning walk and the services of a game ranger. **Directions:** From Belfast take R23, then R540 on a scenic route via Dullstroom to Hoedspruit. Alternatively, fly into Eastgate Airport, Hoedspruit, or Phalaborwa Airport from where you will be collected. Price guide: From R890 per person.

KINGS CAMP

RESERVATIONS: PO BOX 427, NELSPRUIT 1200, NORTHERN PROVINCE
TEL: 27 15 793 3633 FAX: 27 15 793 3634 E-MAIL: kcamp@iafrica.com

This lodge in the heart of the Timbavati Reserve, a mere part of the 2.2 million hectares that combine to form the Kruger National Park, is an idyllic getaway for those searching for a more refined safari adventure. The beautiful open plains are a wealth of diversity, with opportunities to sight those animals, birds, plants and trees for which South Africa is renowned the world over. Kings Camp, comprised of thatched bungalows, is a tribute to bygone days. Colonial refinement is of the essence in this superbly run camp. The rooms are the height of comfort; plush sofas and wicker framework on the beds and chairs, subtly illuminated by the simple lighting create the image of a film set rather than that of a guestroom. Meals are wholesome and

traditional; South African cuisine is served around a fire with a wine cellar that could keep connoisseurs occupied for any length of time. The pool is an intriguing elephant design and joins on to a comfortable viewing deck that overlooks a water hole This place is a paradise for the discerning game enthusiast. **Directions:** Left of N4 (from Jo'burg) at Belfast, follow directions to Dullstroom, Lydenburg, Orighstad then Hoedspruit. There turn right onto R40 for 8km. Left at Kings Camp/Timbavati sign, follow to control gate; there, right at Kings Camp sign, then straight for 2km. Price guide: Rooms R1100–R1750; suite R1450–R2100 including all meals and wildlife activities.

COACH HOUSE

ON THE OLD COACH ROAD AT AGATHA, PO BOX 544, TZANEEN 0850, NORTHERN PROVINCE
TEL: 27 15 307 3641 FAX: 27 15 307 1466 E-MAIL: coachhouse@mweb.co.za

Magnificent mountain scenery, lush green landscape and an outstanding garden surrounded by a working fruit and nut plantation are all colourfully exposed under a sunny, clear blue sky. This is the beautiful, relaxing setting of a hotel which, over 17 years, has built up a reputation for comfort, excellent cuisine, hospitality and service. Within easy reach of the Kruger National Park with its vast array of wild animal and bird life, the Coach House is the only hotel in the Northern Province of South Africa to have a five star grading and has won a number of prestigious awards and accolades. Guests enjoy the choice of 45 luxurious rooms, each having a private balcony overlooking the spectacular Drakensberg mountain range. They are tastefully decorated and furnished with all amenities, including special little extras such as toiletries based on oil of avocado, mineral water bottled at source on the hotel's farm, bowls of fruit and home-baked biscuits. The climate is excellent all year round but the odd chilly winter's evening is warmed by log burning room fires. Diners are spoilt for choice in the attractive restaurant where extensive, imaginative menus are served with flair and aplomb. There is a sauna and fully equipped gym, a billiards and snooker room, floodlit croquet lawn and an 18-hole golf course nearby. **Directions:** From Johannesburg on the N1 and then the R71 to Tzaneen. Price guide: Rooms R375–530 per person.

RÉSIDENCE KLEIN OLIPHANTS HOEK

14 AKADEMIE STREET, FRANSCHHOEK 7690, WESTERN CAPE
TEL: 27 21 876 2566 FAX: 27 21 876 2566 E-MAIL: info@kleinoliphantshoek.com

Built as an English missionary station in 1888, this little gem was a school and then a theatre before assuming its role as a hospitable and comfortable hotel. Tucked away in the French Huguenot village of Franschhoek in a beautiful mountain valley at the heart of the Cape Winelands, it has been renovated to provide a luxurious and restful retreat. Colour, style, charm, ambience and good taste have been delightfully integrated by husband and wife owners Camil and Ingrid Haas. Klein Oliphants Hoek is renowned for the superb cuisine produced by Camil, who trained as a chef at a Michelin Star restaurant in his native Holland. He specialises in innovative and tempting European-African menus, making use of the wide variety of interesting local products. Wines from the surrounding vineyards add to the culinary extravaganza. Summer dining is on the patio or terrace overlooking the solar-heated pool and landscaped garden. In cooler months meals are served in the cosy Victorian living room before a flickering open fire. The seven guest rooms include a luxury suite with a private entrance and garden. All are delightfully and individually decorated, their style enhancing the gentle comfort of the furnishings. Every facility is available, from air conditioning and ceiling fan to TV, hair drier and coffee and tea making tray. **Directions:** From Cape Town, take N1 to exit 47. Then join R45 to Franschhoek. Price guide: Single R375; double/twin R500; suite R650.

GREYTON LODGE

46 MAIN STREET, PO BOX 50, GREYTON 7233
TEL: 27 28 254 9876 FAX: 27 28 254 9672

Built as a trading store in 1882 this fascinating building also served as the village Police Station before assuming its rather more accommodating role as a most comfortable country house hotel. Owners, Philip and Sandra Engelen, have cleverly created this small retreat of cottages nestling in a fertile valley between the Sonderend River and the protective backdrop of the mountains. An unashamedly patriotic display of curios and portraits of royal and political personages can be appreciated from the comfort of a leather Chesterfield creating the illusion of a cosy London Club in the aptly named and convivial 'Royal Bar'. Menus change daily and offer country cuisine, the dining room features a roaring log fire on cooler evenings. Breakfast and lunch may be taken on the terrace overlooking a pretty garden of vines, fruit, trees and roses. Less energetic guests can laze around the swimming pool or enjoy a friendly game of croquet. For the adventurous, there is horse riding, wonderful walks in the hills or a spot of fishing, returning through the quiet gravel streets to admire well-tended rose gardens. **Directions:** Greyton Lodge is only 90 minutes drive from Cape Town via the N2 for 112 km towards Armiston and then 32 km following the exit to Greyton. Price guide (incl. breakfast): Double/twin R310 per person.

BARTHOLOMEUS KLIP FARMHOUSE

PO BOX 36, HERMON 7308, WESTERN CAPE
TEL: 27 22 448 1820 FAX: 27 22 448 1829 E-MAIL: bartholomeus@icon.co.za

Perched on a hillock above a working farm, at the epicentre of a 4,000 hectare private nature reserve, Bartholomeus Klip is a stunningly renovated Victorian farmhouse. Managers Mr. and Mrs. Dupper guarantee a personal and friendly service, a mere 75-minutes drive from bustling Cape Town. The rooms all have en suite bathrooms and there is a spacious verandah to relax in the invigorating country air. The hearty and wonderfully prepared meals reflect the rustic setting and use farm fresh produce. Visitors with an interest in rural life can spend a morning with the shepherds, or drive a combine harvester on the wheat farm. The area is a Natural Heritage Site and guests can observe many flora and animal species unique to the region, chief amongst which is the endangered geometric tortoise, perhaps Africa's rarest reptile. Ideal for mountain biking, hiking, canoeing and windsurfing, the area also gives visitors a taste of traditional South African colonial life, with many quaint villages within easy driving distance. **Directions:** From Cape Town, take the N1 to exit 47. Proceed along the R44 towards Wellington, passing through a 4-way junction after 20 km. Take the Hermon/Ceres turning to your left, and continue for 26 km, and take the Bo Hermon turning to the right. The road to the farmhouse is 2 km on the left, between two white concave walls. Price guide: Rooms from R790–R910 per person sharing.

MIMOSA LODGE

CHURCH STREET, MONTAGU, WESTERN CAPE
TEL: 27 23 614 23 51 FAX: 27 23 614 24 18 E-MAIL: mimosa@lando.co.za

Firmly established in Montagu on the Route 62, this attractive Edwardian National Monument exudes friendliness, comfort and character. It stands back in a quiet side street in the middle of this picturesque historical town. All around are beautifully preserved Georgian, Victorian and Cape Dutch buildings overhung in the distance by the majestic Langeberg mountains. The nine en suite bedrooms are quaint, furnished with period and Art Deco pieces and provide every modern facility. The three generous suites with private patio or balcony offer privacy and are ideal for a longer stay. There are two inviting lounges furnished with Art Deco chairs and sofas, a library and a bar-lounge to relax in or chat with fellow guests. The large garden and apricot orchard enclose a black-marbled salt water pool and provide an endless source for vegetables, fruits and herbs used in the Lodge's highly acclaimed, creative cuisine. Owner and Chef Andreas Küng blends typical South African produce, such as ostrich and karoo lamb, with his European heritage, while excellent wines out of the Lodge's own cellar complement each menu perfectly. Mimosa Lodge is a proud member of The Good Cooks and Their Country Houses. **Directions:** From Cape Town on N1; leave at Worcester and take the Scenic Route 62 towards Oudtshoorn. Price guide (incl. five course gourmet dinner): Single R490; double/twin R375; suite R540–R650.

PALMIET VALLEY ESTATE

PO BOX 9085, KLEIN DRAKENSTEIN, PAARL 7628
TEL: 27 21 862 7741 FAX: 27 21 862 6891 E-MAIL: info@palmiet.co.za

Peace and tranquillity surround this historic homestead which nestles at the foot of the magnificent Drakenstein Mountains. Built in 1692, it has been carefully restored and decorated to its former Cape Dutch style glory. It is idyllically situated at the heart of extensive vineyards in one of the most prolific wine growing areas in the country, just a 30 minutes drive from the beaches, shops, restaurants and entertainment of Cape Town. Comfort and facilities for guests in the manor house match those of the finest accommodation. Each of the 9 en suite bedrooms is individually and thoughtfully furnished with antiques and has all modern amenities from telephone to satellite TV and private safe. All offer panoramic views over the vineyards to the mountains beyond. The restaurant is in authentic period style with heavy furniture and a beamed ceiling, and offers candlelight dining. You'll be invited to experience a taste of the delicate menus, complemented by wines from the estate, in an exclusive setting of antiques, china and crystal. Guests can enjoy a swim in the garden pool or relax on a large terrace. There are 14 golf courses nearby and a chauffeur-driven limousine is available for countryside tours. **Directions:** From Cape Town, leave N1 at Exit 62A towards Nederburg. Turn left after crossing Palmiet River bridge. Alternatively, collection can be made from the airport. Price guide: Available on request.

PONTAC MANOR HOTEL & RESTAURANT

16 ZION STREET, PAARL 7646, WESTERN CAPE
TEL: 27 21 872 0445 FAX: 27 21 872 0460 E-MAIL: pontac@iafrica.com

Grand and luxurious, Pontac Manor dates back to 1723 when the estate was named by its first owner, Pierre de Labuschagne, after his home town in the south of France. Nestling below 'Paarl Rock', the property has been beautifully restored to its original Victorian splendour. Set amidst a large, scultped garden with pool, the manor house is delightfully decorated with a charming eclectic mix of antique furniture and interesting African artefacts and offers 10 spacious, air-conditioned double bedrooms. The old wine cellar has been stylishly converted into another five self-contained executive rooms with Spanish reed ceilings. There is also a superb Honeymoon Suite, complete with king-size bed and Jacuzzi bath.

All the rooms are en suite and equipped to the highest standards. On the wide Victorian verandah, guests can sip a sundowner while savouring the magnificent view over the valley to the mountains beyond, or they can choose between two comfortable lounges and a bar. The newly opened 'fine dining' restaurant pampers the palate with local and international specialities. For executive meetings in an exclusive setting, the boardroom and new conference suite are the ideal venue. **Directions:** From Cape Town take the N1 to Paarl. Pontac Estate is just off the main road in the centre of town. Price guide: Single from R345; double (per person sharing) from R256; suite R704–R880.

d'OUWE WERF

30 CHURCH STREET, STELLENBOSCH, 7600 WESTERN CAPE
TEL: 27 21 887 4608 FAX: 27 21 887 4626 E-MAIL: ouwewerf@iafrica.com

Conveniently positioned in the heart of historic Stellenbosch, the d'Ouwe Werf is a renovated Georgian style hideaway which dates from 1802, making it South Africa's oldest surviving Inn. Now a national monument, the hotel has housed many famous guests, with Sir George Grey noting the quality of its service as far back as 1860. The 25 bedrooms are all spacious, each with its own character and appeal, tastefully furnished with exquisite antiques and fully equipped with modern facilities. The traditional food, served in an elegant dining room, is typical of the Western Cape region and visitors should avail of the excellent cellar, boasting the finest wines from the renowned local vineyards. As South Africa's second oldest town, Stellenbosch is the ideal location to soak in the history of the country. Its architecture reflects South Africa's Dutch heritage, and the many museums in the vicinity would slake the appetite of the most curious of history lovers. With rugged mountain ranges encasing the town, visitors can also bask in the tranquillity of the many valleys and rivers in the surrounding area. D'Ouwe Werf staff can organise balloon safaris, mountain biking and historical and wine tours of Stellenbosch. Guests can sunbathe by the pool, hidden in a private courtyard. **Directions:** Take the N2 out of Cape Town and turn left at exit 33. Continue to Stellenbosch along the R310. Price guide: Rooms from R385–R520 per person.

LANZERAC MANOR AND WINERY

PO. BOX 4, STELLENBOSCH, WESTERN CAPE
TEL: 2721 887 1132 FAX: 2721 887 2310 E-MAIL: info@lanzerac.co.za

This fine example of Cape Dutch architecture was built 300 years ago and is the essence of opulence. Considered by many to be the Cape Wine Route's best-kept secret, the property is situated within a 155 hectare working wine estate. Rich furnishings and fabrics adorn the 48 spacious rooms, each opening out onto private patios which afford glorious views across the Helderberg Mountains. The two suites and Royal Pool Suite, with its own private swimming pool, are truly luxuriant. The property will delight gastronomes as it excels in culinary standards. The Sunday buffet lunch at The Governors Restaurant must not be missed whilst Mediterranean-style dishes are served alfresco in the Lady Anne Courtyard. Those seeking a more informal ambience may enjoy a Cape country speciality at The Terrace, the only restaurant in the region with a view over Table Mountain. Wine connoisseurs must indulge in the full cellar tour and sample old favourites such as Cabernet Sauvignon and Merlot as well as the new De Forellen range. Worldwide shipping can be arranged for any purchases. Mountain hikes, golfing and mountain biking are available for the energetic whilst more leisurely pastimes include lazing by the many swimming pools or exploring the lush gardens. **Directions:** 30 minutes from the centre of Cape Town; the nearest motorway is the N1. Price guide: Rooms R620–R1465; suite R1185–R3435.

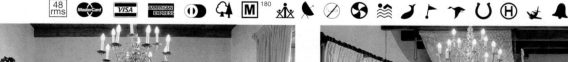

LYNGROVE COUNTRY HOUSE

PO BOX 7275, STELLENBOSCH 7599
TEL: 27 21 842 2116 FAX: 27 21 842 2118 E-MAIL: lyngrove@iafrica.com

Lyngrove is a well presented, comfortably proportioned country house, bordered by its own vines at the heart of the Stellenbosch wine region. Spacious en suite bathrooms complement the luxurious bedrooms named after the classic grape varieties of wine produced in the area. The Sauvignon Blanc Room is described thus: "Garden suite, where floral notes mesh with grassy overtones". There are others, equally enticing to choose from! A stroll across the terrace with its expanse of terracotta tiles leads to the swimming pool and a shady garden bar framed in the near distance by the Helderberg Mountains. There is an ambience of tranquillity and of calm created by the thoughtful choice of colours and fabrics in the welcoming sitting room and throughout the house. Wine lovers will feel thoroughly at home here and local cellar tours and tastings are abundant. Horse riding, mountain biking, hiking trails and historical walks can be enjoyed. Trout and deep sea fishing can also be arranged or a romantic picnic for two on the beach. **Directions**: Lyngrove is only 30 minutes from Cape Town. Take the N2 from Cape Town towards Somerset West and exit on the R44 to Winery Road at Firgrove Macassar. Or the N1 to Paarl exiting at the R304 through Stellenbosch. Price guide (incl. breakfast): Rooms from R475 per person.

RIVER MANOR

NUMBER 6, THE AVENUE, PO BOX 3190 MATIELAND, 7602 STELLENBOSCH, WESTERN CAPE
TEL: 27 21 887 9944 FAX: 27 21 887 9940 E-MAIL: rivermanor@adept.co.za

River Manor, built in the early 1900s, is situated in a quiet oak-lined avenue across from the Eerste River. It is a mere two minutes' stroll from the historic village centre with its many restaurants, museums and art galleries and only a forty minutes' drive from Cape Town. With its understated luxury and antique furnishings, River Manor offers traditional Cape hospitality and personal service, a celebration of gracious living. The eight luxurious rooms are decorated within the theme of "Colonial charm with a touch of Africa" and combine old-world charm with modern conveniences. From port and sherry trays to soft towelling bathrobes, attention to detail provides for luxury and comfort. Two garden suites open out onto the attractive swimming pool set in the secluded, perfectly manicured garden, which is vibrant with lush greenery and responding colours. Enjoy leisurely Colonial poolside breakfasts, before exploring the historical university town of Stellenbosch and its surrounding winelands. As a perfect complement, picnic baskets are available upon request. At the end of the day, guests may enjoy watching the sun set behind the Simonsberg Mountain, whilst sipping cocktails on the upstairs terrace. **Directions:** Follow the N1 from Cape Town or the N2 from airport, take exits leading to Stellenbosch. Price guide: Rooms R400, suite R550 per person sharing including a full English and health breakfast. Single rates on request.

ZANDBERG FARM

PO BOX 5337, SOMERSET WEST, STELLENBOSCH WINE ROUTE 7135, WESTERN CAPE
TEL & FAX: 27 21 842 2945 E-MAIL: info@zandberg.co.za

Zandberg is a beautiful working wine farm estate encompassed by its own vines at the heart of the renowned Stellenbosch wine region. Peaceful and calm, it is a perfect little paradise just 30 minutes from Cape Town and 5 minutes from False Bay with its shopping mall. There are magnificent views over the vineyards towards Table Mountain from the guest house and 11 Cape Colonial cottages, situated in exquisite gardens. Each self-catering cottage has a private entrance and garden terrace, is delightfully decorated and furnished with every modern comfort. Some have open fireplaces in front of which to relax over a drink on cooler evenings. With a constantly changing menu, dining is a delight. The informal but elegant award-winning restaurant provides excellent traditional and international cuisine, complemented by a superb wine list. Champagne breakfasts are served beneath the garden's shady oak trees or in the thatched breakfast room. Guests meet for sundowners between 6 - 7. There is also a popular barbecue area and 'honesty' bar. Guests can enjoy relaxing in or around the swimming pool, whale watching from the shore at False Bay, golf at the nearby Erinvale Club, winery visits and exploring historic Stellenbosch, South Africa's second oldest town. **Directions:** 20 mins from Cape Town airport. Take N2 towards Somerset West and take exit 43 onto R44 towards Stellenbosch, Winery Road is a turning on the left. Price guide: Rooms R260–R500.

RIJK'S COUNTRY HOUSE

PO BOX 340, TULBAGH 6820

TEL: 27 23 2301006 FAX: 27 23 2301125 E-MAIL: bookings@rijks.co.za

The charming village of Tulbagh is renowned for its Cape Dutch and Victorian architecture and boasts South Africa's densest concentration of National Monuments. Whilst the village is a haven for heritage enthusiasts, the area also welcomes many visitors each year for its other speciality – wine, which is a very important criterion at Rijk's Ridge. Surrounded by the imposing Witzenberg and Winterhoek mountains, the country house and wine estate has built its own wine cellar, launching a first range of wines this year. There are 10 rooms with twin beds and showers and 2 honeymoon suites with en suite baths and showers. The 3 self-contained de luxe cottages overlook an attractive lake. All rooms are light and airy with high ceilings and fans for the summer months. Guests may admire the beautiful scenery from the lounge or enjoy a refreshing beverage in the cocktail bar. Fine country cuisine is prepared in the restaurant, and nature lovers may dine alfresco on the lakeside terrace. Take a dip in the outdoor pool or practise golf, fishing and horse-riding nearby. There are numerous walking and cycling trails within easy reach; guided tours of the fruit farms can be arranged. A new conference centre has been built for business requirements. **Directions:** Take R44 off N1, turn off at Wellington, R44 to Tulbagh, Rijk's Ridge Country House is 2kms through the village. Price guide (pp. inc. full English breakfast): Rooms R278–R358; suite R328–R438; cottages from R195 per person.

WESTERN CAPE
THE GARDEN ROUTE

UNIONDALE

AVONTUUR

Prince Alfred Pass

DE VLUG

OUTENIQUA MTNS

Keurbooms River Nature Reserve

98

Outeniqua Pass

RUITERBOS

Montagu Pass

BLANCO

GEORGE

BARRINGTON

WILDERNESS

SOUTANNI

NATURES VALLEY

99

100 102 104

KNYSNA

103

PLETTENBERG BAY

106

GROOT BRAKRIVIER

HARTENBOS

HEROLDSBAAI

SEDGEFIELD

Nature & Marine Reserve

95

94 96

101

105

CAPE SEAL

ROBBERG NATURE RESERVE

97

MOSSEL BAY

The Head

INDIAN OCEAN

93

BELVIDERE MANOR

PO BOX 1195, KNYSNA 6570, WESTERN CAPE
TEL: 27 44 387 1055 FAX: 27 44 387 1059 E-MAIL: manager@belvidere.co.za

Belvidere Manor is a piece of Cape Georgian history. A grand, luxurious establishment dating back to 1834 and now proclaimed a National Monument. It is a haven of beauty and tranquillity where guests can unwind, relax and enjoy fine views over the blue waters of the nearby Knysna Lagoon. Accommodation is in neat, single, double or three-bedroomed whitewalled cottages throughout the grounds. Each is sumptuously furnished and tastefully decorated. They are all en suite, have a fully fitted kitchen, telephone, a comfortable living room with open fire and a wide verandah from where sundowners can be enjoyed as dusk descends over the lush garden surrounds. The chef creates excellent gourmet and imaginative menus in the restaurant,

awarded a blazon by the Chaine des Rotisseurs, where the yellowwood and a candlelit ambiance enriches the Manor's sense of sophistication and luxury. Breakfast can be taken on the long verandah of Belvidere House and a leisurely lunch in the garden's shady gazebo. A tavern housed in a recently restored original farmhouse is a particularly popular rendezvous for both visitors and locals. For the energetic guests, there is a large swimming pool, tennis, golf, fishing and horse riding can be arranged and boat trips can be taken on the tranquil lagoon. **Directions:** The Manor is just off the N2 National Road between George and Plettenberg Bay. Price guide (incl. breakfast): Rooms from R440–R840 per person sharing.

FALCONS VIEW MANOR

PO BOX 3083, KNYSNA 6570, GARDEN ROUTE WESTERN CAPE
TEL: 27 44 382 6767 FAX: 27 44 382 6430 E-MAIL: falcons@pixie.co.za

This exclusive Cape Victorian country house stands above the Kynsna Lagoon offering superb views from its gracious sitting rooms, intimate guest bar and covered verandahs. Surrounded by magnificent gardens and woodlands, it is a comfortable stroll from shops, restaurants and galleries. Dating back to the late 19th century, Falcons View Manor is a luxurious establishment with beautiful architectural detail, original period fittings, high ceilings and lounges with fine furnishings. This National Monument is excellently run by an award-winning team who give the highest level of personal service, cuisine and comfort, creating an atmosphere of tranquillity where guests may relax in informal, yet elegant, surroundings. The spacious en suite bedrooms overlook gardens or lagoon and are equipped with air conditioning, TV and telephone, extra length beds, fine linen and plush duvets. The lovely garden suites have vaulted ceilings with french doors onto private terraces with beautiful views. Delicious breakfasts are served on the sunny garden patio, lunch can be enjoyed beside the pool and superb evening meals are served either in the sophisticated dining room or outside under the stars. Beaches, golf, tennis, horse riding and fishing nearby. **Directions:** From N2 in Knysna 3rd left from George – 4th light right from Plettenberg, follow signs. Price guide: High Seasons Rooms R880–R1190; suites R1280.

MILKWOOD BAY GUEST HOUSE

PO BOX 179, KNYSNA 6570, WESTERN CAPE
TEL: 27 44 384 0092 FAX: 27 44 384 1120 E-MAIL: milkbay@milkwood.co.za

Modern, stylish and relaxing, Milkwood is a luxury, up-market Mediterranean-style guesthouse situated on the Eastern Head of the lovely Knysna Lagoon. The angular exterior with its huge picture windows and shady balconies drops straight down to the sandy fringe of blue water that attracts sun lovers and watersports enthusiasts alike. A personal warm welcome awaits every visitor to this friendly, delightful and restful escape from a busy, noisy world, offering peace and tranquillity. Rates are for bed and breakfast only but there are many excellent restaurants in the town and plenty of shops to sample and enjoy. The five bedrooms reflect the comfortable ambience of the house; each is en suite, cool and welcoming, individually furnished and decorated and has every modern comfort from underfloor heating to satellite television. All look out over the lagoon to the distant, deep green mountain range. Guests can start the day with a healthy breakfast, then visit the town's attractions or seek more adventurous explorations on walks and hikes over the surrounding countryside. Milkwood has a large indoor heated swimming pool, complete with sauna, and there is tennis, golf, fishing and horse riding within walking distance. Also popular are boat trips on the lagoon. **Directions:** From N2 between George and Plettenberg turn onto George Rex Drive and drive towards The Heads. Price guide: Double R295–R685 per person sharing.

REIN'S COASTAL NATURE RESERVE

PO BOX 298, ALBERTINIA 6695
TEL: 27 28 735 3322 FAX: 27 28 735 3324 E-MAIL: info@reinsouthafrica.com

Here at Rein's Coastal Nature Reserve, a mere stone's throw away from Cape Town and Port Elizabeth, nature has provided a majestic setting for a reserve that offers a score of activities whilst remaining at one with the infinite beauty that surrounds. From this remarkable vantage point, one may experience first hand the hauntingly melodious songs of the whales as zebras idly amble along the shore. Mirroring the subtle earth tones favoured by the Khoisin hunter-gatherers that once roamed the region, the rooms are warm and comforting with luxurious furniture and ample space. For those wishing to commune one on one with nature, the tranquil, refined Fisherman's Cottages, though still fully functional, remain secluded such that a hermit-like lifestyle may be pursued with ease. At Reins, visitors may walk through the 'fynbos' vegetation that shrouds the land, or stroll along Boulder Beach where the waves gently bath the shoreline. A myriad of activities is available, from snorkelling to star gazing, from mountain biking to fly fishing, there is something to please both the energetic and the lazy. In Reins, guests may travel back to the time of their ancestors, experiencing nature as they knew it, yet in all the comfort the 20th century can provide. **Directions:** From Cape Town, take N2, turn right onto R325 towards Gouritzmond. Follow road for 18km, turn right towards Still Bay; follow road for 8km, entrance on left. Price guide: Rooms from R260.

ROSENHOF COUNTRY HOUSE

264 BARON VAN REEDE STREET, OUDTSHOORN, WESTERN CAPE, SOUTH AFRICA
TEL: +27 44 2791 791 FAX: +27 44 2791 793 E-MAIL: rosenhof@xsinet.co.za

Owners Nic and Ferda Barrow have carefully restored this stylish Victorian house which sits just on the outskirts of Oudtshoorn. One of the very best hotels in the area, Rosenhof is named after the beautiful rose and herb filled garden. With yellow wood beams and ceilings and open fireplaces, several lovely sitting rooms provide the perfect place to relax before or after dinner. Guests can admire the work of well-known South African artists on display. Traditional home-cooked country cuisine with a cordon bleu touch is prepared by Ferda and her team, and Nic's wine collection includes some unusual bottles. Each of the 12 rooms is furnished individually in Cape-Victorian style, and all have TV and air conditioning.

Another welcome addition is the hotel pool, where visitors can enjoy a refreshing dip. Your hosts are more than happy to recommend sightseeing tours, and there is much to experience in the surrounding area. Local wine estates, museums, nature trails, ostrich and crocodile farms are well worth a visit, as are the nearby Cango Caves. Golf and horse riding can be arranged, and a trip over the spectacular Swartberg Pass and back via Meiringspoort is a must. Private functions may be held in the gazebo, and Rosenhof also offers excellent conference facilities in its old wagon-house. **Directions:** N2 Cape Town to Port Elizabeth. Take turnoff at George. Price guide: Single R410; Double R350–450 per person.

Hog Hollow Country Lodge

PO BOX 503, PLETTENBERG BAY, WESTERN CAPE 6600
TEL: 27 44 534 8879 FAX: 27 44 534 8879 E-MAIL: hoghollow@global.co.za

A trip to this private nature reserve is like visiting an Eden-like sanctuary. Surrounded by an imposing mountain range and deep gorges, Hog Hollow provides discerning travellers with the perfect location to appreciate nature. Owners Andy and Debbie create a convivial and earthy atmosphere where traditional farm house breakfasts are served on a wooden deck overlooking the forest, while sumptuous evening meals are taken around a candlelit communal table. Each of the 12 individual rooms offers a private deck with a hammock, overlooking the indigenous forests and Tsitsikamma Mountains. Situated 18 km east of the picturesque town of Plettenberg Bay, Hollow Hog Country Lodge is considered an ideal base for exploring the magnificent Garden Route. Nature conservationists take guided walks, with the Otter, Outeniqua and Tsitsikamma trails the most popular hikes in the region. The area is also renowned for the beauty and variety of its flora and monkeys, baboons and leopards are seen in the vicinity. Guests can also experience the unique thrill of whale and dolphin watching in the Bay. **Directions:** 18 km east of Plettenberg Bay, along the N2 towards Port Elizabeth. Take the Hog Hollow/Barnyard turnoff down Askop Road. The lodge is on the left hand side of the road. Price Guide: Rooms R440–R660 per person.

KURLAND

PO BOX 209, THE CRAGS 6602, WESTERN CAPE
TEL: 27 44 534 8082 FAX: 27 44 534 8699 E-MAIL: dkurland@mweb.co.za

This is a stunning holiday retreat in a perfect location. A beautiful Cape Dutch style home, it has everything the discerning traveller could wish for. Style, elegance and luxurious comfort. Kurland is excellent in every respect and superb value for money. The attractive, sparkling white rambling building stands in the heart of a vast, open landscape in the shadow of a magnificent mountain range tipped with frothy white clouds. Views all round are breathtaking. Inside is tranquillity, coolness and light, restful décor, beamed ceilings, open fires, fine furniture and rich furnishings. Nothing is too much trouble for friendly owners Peter and Dianne Behr who actively encourage guests to relax and feel completely at home. The eight en suite guestrooms are individually and delightfully decorated, spacious and complete with fireplace, satellite TV, telephone, and hairdryer, bathrobes and mini bar. Four have plunge pools and six have loft bedrooms with bathrooms specially catering for children. Sumptuous meals are served in the charming, intimate dining room or the piazza. There is a health spa with swimming pool, steam bath, sauna, gym and plunge pool as well as a tennis court. Riding can be arranged. A polo complex with 36 stables and four polo fields form part of the estate. Sailing, whale and dolphin watching at Plettenberg Bay can be organised. **Directions:** Kurland is 19kms from Plettenberg Bay on N2. Price guide: Double R950–R1500.

LAIRD'S LODGE

PO BOX 657, PLETTENBERG BAY 6600, WESTERN CAPE
TEL: 27 4453 27721 FAX: 27 4453 27671 E-MAIL: info@lairdslodge.co.za

A mere stone's throw away from Plettenburg Bay, Laird's Lodge is a stunningly refurbished Cape Dutch style home that promises the friendliest of service in a most idyllic location. Set in its own 24-acre estate, the Lodge offers breath-taking mountain views, a spacious swimming pool, and the chance to amble in beautifully maintained gardens. The high-ceilinged bedrooms combine elegance and charm with comfortable and spacious accommodation, and owners Alison and Murray Brebner promise an unparalleled level of service in warm and relaxed surroundings. The sumptuous and imaginative cuisine reflects the attention to detail that typifies Laird's Lodge. Blending the authenticity of South African cooking and the principles of nouvelle cuisine, the fare is simply divine, and visitors should not miss the specialities of the house - freshly caught seafood and succulent venison. Laird's Lodge is uniquely positioned for exploring the seemingly endless series of golden beaches and rugged hillocks that the Garden Route region is famed for. Chief amongst the nearby attractions is undoubtedly the whale and dolphin watching trips that the lodge organises. World class golf courses abound and the Robberg Nature and Marine Reserve and the Tsitsikama National Park are a short drive away. **Directions:** Laird's Lodge is 8km for Plattenburg Bay and 20 km from Knysna at the heart of the renowned Garden Route. Price guide: Double R300–R400 per person.

THE LODGE ON THE BAY

77 BEACHY HEAD DRIVE, PO BOX 206, PLETTENBERG BAY 6600, WESTERN CAPE
TEL: 27 44 533 4724 FAX: 27 44 533 2681 E-MAIL: info@thelodge.co.za

Plettenberg Bay embraces a glorious sweep of coastal scenery. Edged east to west by sandy beaches, overshadowed by mountain ranges and protected seawards by the Robberg Nature Reserve's rocky peninsula it is a glamorous holiday destination in the heart of the Garden Route. The Lodge on the Bay is a stunning hotel situated on the 4km long Robberg Beach just east of the Reserve. It is the serene, modern retreat dream of owners Siegfried and Yvette Kopp, whose Buddhist philosophy is expressed subtly throughout the lodge. The contrasting textures and muted colours, raw silks, sisal, chenille, velvet, unpolished marble, smooth linens and crisp cotton reflect the natural outside beauty and soothe the mind. The Lodge's simple façade gives the impression of a small building, but inside are four levels which open onto large open-plan spaces featuring glass sliding doors and picture windows that afford panoramic sea and mountain views. The first level contains sitting and dining areas, guest rooms and pool deck, and a few steps lead up to more guest rooms. Another level has a spa, sauna and a luxurious Zen suite with plunge pool and private garden. All guest rooms are en suite, and beautifully furnished. Breakfasts and light lunches are served on the pool deck overlooking the bay. Whales and dolphins can be spotted from the rooftop garden! **Directions:** From Cape Town on the N2. Price guide: Double R850–2000.

MILKWOOD MANOR

LOOKOUT BEACH, PLETTENBERG BAY 6600, WESTERN CAPE
TEL: 27 44 533 0420 FAX: 27 44 533 0921 E-MAIL: info@milkwood-manor.co.za

With its yellow frontage, white framed windows and ornate roof balustrade, Milkwood Manor (featured below) is a welcoming sight to visitors seeking relaxation and clean, fresh sea air in one of South Africa's premier destinations. Set in the heart of the Garden Route, Plettenberg is backdropped by the Outeniqua and Tsitsikamma mountain ranges, awash with rivers and lagoons, lush with indigenous forests and bounded by magnificent sandy beaches, including the glamorous Lookout Beach. The Manor, with its spectacular views over the Keurbooms River mouth, Keurbooms Lagoon and a natural bird sanctuary, is just a 2 minute leisurely stroll from the beach and 10 minutes from the seaside village with its shops and sophisticated restaurants. Opened in September 1999, this elegant hotel with its distinctive, colonial look has a cool and stylishly decorated interior. Twelve en suite guestrooms offer every comfort from colour TV to tea and coffee making facilities. The cosy lounge features an open fire and the top deck commands panoramic views. Guests can laze around a large pool after a day exploring the countryside or enjoying a multitude of sports. When there is sufficient demand, classic Thai dishes are served in an intimate dining room or al fresco. **Directions:** Plettenberg Bay is on the N2. 220kms west of Port Elizabeth and 550km east of Cape Town. Price guide: Double: R280–R420 per person sharing.

MALLARD RIVER LODGE

PO BOX 532, PLETTENBERG BAY 6600, WESTERN CAPE
TEL: 27 44 533 2982 FAX: 27 44 535 9336 E-MAIL: mallard@pixie.co.za

The 180° views that greet you on arrival at Mallard River Lodge are a surprise and a delight. The Bitou valley stretches out to east and west with shimmering wetlands and a twisting river where otters and water birds make their homes. A warm welcome will assure you that you have chosen a wonderful place to stay! Each room is a separate building and on entering, you'll be enchanted by the restful décor, the sitting area with fireplace and by the attention to detail. In the bathroom, the tub lies under a large picture window so that you may gaze at the magnificent view while taking a bath. A private balcony with reclining deck chairs will provide total contentment as you soak in the African sunshine. Sublimely delicious, innovative dinners and excellent local wines will complete pleasurable evenings. The lodge is a tranquil and private place, yet it is a mere 4 km from Plettenberg Bay with its exceptional restaurants, shops and beaches. Visit with ease the entire Garden Route from the towns of Oudtshoorn and Knysna, to the spectacular coastlines of the Tzitzikamma National Park. Nearby, whale and dolphin trips, golf, water sports and more are easily arranged. Aromatherapy and massages can be organised in the privacy of your room. **Directions:** 2 kilometres past Plettenberg Bay on the N2 towards Port Elizabeth, then left into Rietvlei Road. Price guide: Double R295–R490 per person sharing (including breakfast).

PLETTENBERG PARK

PO BOX 167, PLETTENBERG BAY, WESTERN CAPE 6600
TEL: 27 44 533 9067 FAX: 27 44 533 9092 E-MAIL: info@plettenbergpark.co.za

Plettenberg Park is described in one prestigious book as 'having the most spectacular setting in the whole of South Africa', and in another as 'a place of peace, love, space and tranquillity'. This beautiful clifftop retreat is stunning. Situated within the most exclusive private nature reserve in the Cape it stands high on the majestic cliffs of a dramatically beautiful coastline. From the front, guests have spectacular views over the Indian Ocean. The rear overlooks the calm lakeshore of an inland wild duck sanctuary and the sprawling indigenous vegetation. Plettenberg park is an all-weather hotel, swathed in sunshine during the summer and equally splendid in winter when log fires provide warmth. The interior is refreshingly simple with fine furniture and furnishings and an understated Afro-Colonial décor that uses only natural materials in earthy tones and crisp whites. Ceilings are high, there are wall-to-wall windows and wide, shady terraces. The 4 en suite bedrooms have every home-from-home comfort and offer breathtaking views. Dining is a delight. Cuisine is excellent and beautifully served after the chef has discussed the menu with guests and prepared each request individually. The hotel has a pool and a private beach with a tidal rock pool where guests can swim and snorkel. Sailing, water skiing or fishing can also be arranged. **Directions:** From Cape Town on the N2 towards Port Elizabeth. Price guide: Double R850–R1660 per person sharing.

PALMS WILDERNESS

NO. 1 OWEN GRANT STREET, WILDERNESS 6560, WESTERN CAPE
TEL: 27 44 877 1420 FAX: 27 44 877 1422 E-MAIL: palms@pixie.co.za

This attractive, thatched roof guest house is perfect for those who are looking for a personal touch when on holiday. Service is impeccable and attentive with nothing too much trouble for Swiss owners and managers Chris, Italo, Tom and Urs. With Swiss, French, German, Italian and English spoken, international visitors are well catered for. Palms stands in lush tropical gardens in the heart of Wilderness almost midway between Cape Town and Port Elizabeth and just 50kms west of Knysna. It edges onto a phenomenal lake area and the magnificent, unspoilt Wilderness Beach, from where whales and dolphins can be viewed. A stay here is guaranteed to be memorable and relaxing, and great attention has been paid to décor and

furnishings. All 12 bedrooms have private entrances leading into the garden and a black marbled pool area. Each is en suite, has stylish ethnic furnishings, a single or queen-sized bed and every home-from-home comfort and facility, including Satellite television and safe deposit. Excellent and imaginative cuisine reflects the attention to detail that typifies Palms. Light snacks and drinks can be enjoyed on the shady verandah and by the pool. Guests can walk forest trails, fish, paraglide, mountain bike and play golf, ride a steam train from George or shop in Plettenberg Bay. **Directions:** From Cape Town, take the N2 and leave at Wilderness turnoff. Price guide: Single R375–R410; double R285–R375 per person sharing.

ZAMBIA

REPUBLIC OF
THE CONGO

TANZANIA

ZAKEMWERA

MBALA

LUWINGU

KASAMA

LUSENGA National Park

Lake Bangweulu

Swamps

ANGOLA

S'OLWEZI

MANSA

MUCHINGA

LUNDAZI

CHINGOLA

MUFULIRA

NDOLA

MTS

108

110

KITWE

LUANSHYA

109

MALAWI

ZAMBEZI

CHIPATA

R. Zambezi

KABWE

MULUNGUSHI

MONGU

LUSAKA

MOZAMBIQUE

LIUWA
PLAIN

Kariba Dam

NAMBIA

NANGWESHI

KAFUE NATIONAL
PARK

Sioma Ngwesi
National Park

Lake Kariba

CAPRIVI
STRIP

LIVINGSTONE

ZIMBABWE

VICTORIA FALLS

BOTSWANA

CHIBEMBE CAMP

PRIVATE BAG 286X, RIDGEWAY, LUSAKA, ZAMBIA
TEL: 260 1 265814 FAX: 260 1 262291 E-MAIL: info@chilongozi.com

Chibembe Tented Lodge is the camp furthest north in the South Luangwa National Park. As the main activity here is walking, a paddle across the river in canoes brings guests into the National Park. Walks are conducted with fully qualified and experienced guides who have a thorough knowledge of the Luangwa Valley. Game drives are an option in the Nsefu Sector – approximately 20 minutes drive from the lodge. Accommodation is in enormous tents; each is well secluded from the others to provide maximum privacy. The huge hexagonal shaped tents open on 3 sides allowing the feeling of the bush inside. Afternoon siestas are spent on blissfully comfortable beds looking out through the canopy of enormous trees over the Chibembe Channel.

The enormous bathrooms are open-roofed areas with reed walls, whilst the 'mess' area is simply furnished with comfortable and stylish pieces. The tea table is always laid and a jug of ice cold fresh lemon juice – Chibembe's secret recipe – is always ready to be poured. Superb meals are served at Chibembe: fabulous brunches are waiting for guests after a long morning walk and wonderful three-course dinners are served under the enormous canopy of acacia and mahogany trees. The lodge is closed between November and May.
Directions: 12 minutes by charter plane from Mfuwe, or a 2 hours road transfer through National Park and sparsely inhabited land. Price guide (fully inclusive): Single US$350; double US$250 per person.

PAMUSHANA

MALILANGWE PRIVATE WILDLIFE RESERVE, RESERVATIONS: PO BOX MP845 MOUNT PLEASANT, HARARE, ZIMBABWE
TEL: 263 4 722983 or 263 4 725797/9 FAX: 263 4 735530 E-MAIL: mctsales@africaonline.co.zw

Perched on a precipice overlooking the Malilangwe lake and surrounding bush, this luxurious lodge combines the isolation of impenetrable wilderness with the luxury and comfort of five-star accommodation. As the visitor enters Pamushana, built entirely with local materials and covered with African thatching, one is immediately struck by the shimmering pool of incandescent water which appears to melt into the lake beyond. The sumptuous meals are served in a circular dining room, whose walls are covered by frescoes displaying the savage beauty of the African bush. Visitors may also dine on a verandah with panoramic views of the lake. Each air-conditioned villa has a game-viewing balcony, complete with Swarovski telescope and contains stone work and rich works of art from the region. Situated on the Malilangwe Private Wildlife Reserve, the Lodge offers game drives and walks tailored to visitors' interests, night bush drives and visits to the nearby bushman paintings. The Malilangwe Reserve is famous for the diversity of its wildlife and with over 400 species of birds, it is a haven for ornithologists. The stunning Gonarezhou National Park is also in the vicinity, as are three golf courses. **Directions:** Pamushana is a 35 minute drive from Chiredzi and 3 hours from Beit Bridge. Price guide: Rooms Single US$600; double/twin US$480 per person per night. Contact our reservations office for seasonal specials.

MEIKLES HOTEL

**PO BOX 594, CORNER JASON MOYO, THIRD STREET, HARARE, ZIMBABWE
TEL: 263 4 707721/251705 FAX: 263 4 707754/3 E-MAIL: meikles@internet.co.zw**

Overlooking the beautiful Africa Unity Square gardens, The Meikles Hotel provides its visitors with an old-fashioned service, and it has done since it opened in 1915. Providing the perfect combination of business and pleasure, the Meikles Hotel is situated conveniently within the City Business Centre. All business facilities, secretarial, fax, E-mail and Internet – to mention but a few – are available in the business centre, and the conference rooms can hold up to 250 delegates. After a hard day of meetings, the famous Explorers Club Bar is the perfect place to unwind and soak up the ambience of the traditional décor. You will have a difficult time choosing between the hotel's three superb restaurants. La Fontaine serves exceptional meals during an evening of dance with a live band; the Pavilion Restaurant and Coffee Bar offer both indoor and outdoor dining, and the Bagatelle Restaurant is famous for its cuisine of the highest standard. Harare is a fascinating city with a colourful array of things to do. Enjoy a day strolling around the crafts markets or visit the botanical and sculpture gardens, art galleries, museums and Parliament Buildings. The more adventurous may go on a safari bush trail or take a ride on an elephant along the Manyame River. **Directions:** Price guide: Rooms US$210; double/twin US$240; suite US$375.

THE HIDE SAFARI CAMP

HWANGE NATIONAL PARK, ZIMBABWE
TEL: 263 4 660554/6 FAX: 263 4 621216 E-MAIL: presgrou@mail.pci.co.zw

This is a spectacular and unique African experience far removed from viewing the wild from the windows of a mini-bus. The Hide is situated within the magnificent Hwange National Park, not only home to the 'big five' but having one of Africa's highest game populations. Professionally guided walks or game drives, tailor-made to suit individual requirements, will provide the best "wildlife experience" Africa can offer. Our underground hides and platforms afford you safe close quarter photographic opportunities. Accommodation is in luxury East African style tents, comfortably furnished, each with en suite shower and toilet facilities. Relax on your porch and view the game that frequent the camp's waterhole. When darkness falls, the nocturnal species are gently illuminated by a diffused light. The central feature is a large thatch 'A' frame with an upstairs lounge and open viewing deck offering superb views. Fine cuisine is served in a homely atmosphere with everyone seated around a large teak table, where guests share the day's experiences. An evening meal is made even more memorable by a herd of elephants quenching their thirst. After an optional spotlit night drive, allow the calls of the wild to serenade you to a good night's sleep. **Directions:** One of the camp's professional guides will meet guests at Hwange airport or Hwange Safari Lodge and transfer them on a slow one hour's drive through the park in one of the game viewing land rovers. Price guide: on application.

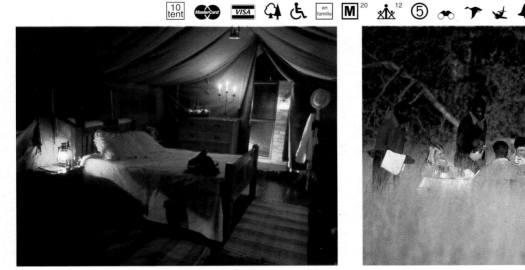

SANYATI LODGE

RESERVATIONS: PO BOX CY3371, CAUSEWAY, HARARE, ZIMBABWE
TEL: 263 4 701732 FAX: 263 4 701737 E-MAIL: sanyati@icon.co.zw

A 50 minute powerboat ride across Lake Kariba brings guests to Sanyati Lodge, a large stone and thatch structure, and spread out amongst large indigenous trees, individual lodges. Welcoming smiles from Sanyati staff assisting with the docking of the boat in the small harbour, shortly followed by an ice-cold cocktail set the scene of indulgence to come. The exquisitely decorated lodges with huge mosquito nets draped over the beds and wonderful photographs of the pioneer days transpose guests to a bygone era. Large bathrooms feature claw-foot baths below enormous glass windows and a glass door leading to an outdoor shower from where the African skies can be appreciated. The living room is sumptuously furnished with natural fabrics and African artefacts. Backgammon and solitaire, as well as local games, are played from comfortable sofas whilst sipping coffee and liqueurs after dinner. Meals are served from an open dining room above the pool and bar area. Breakfasts and lunches are buffet-style. Attentive staff answer their guests every request, yet still create a friendly ambience. Guides are of an exceptionally high standard and activities include drives and walks in the Matusadona National Park, fishing for the renowned tiger fish or delicious bream, which the chef will prepare, or game viewing by boat. **Directions:** By motorboat from Kariba Town. Price guide (fully inclusive): Single US$450; double/twin US$350 suite US$390–US$550.

ROYAL KINGDOM LODGE

PO BOX AC891, ASCOT, BULAWAYO, MOTPOS, ZIMBABWE
TEL: 263 11 401 446 FAX: 263 9 60662 E-MAIL: royalk@byo.internet.co.zw

Perched above some of the oldest and most dramatic rock formations in the world, Royal Kingdom Lodge offers an evocative African experience complete with elegant colonial charm. Set within its own private nature reserve, the lodge caters for 12 guests in six individual en suite rooms, all with lounge and private patio. The thatched chalets are connected to the central lodge by raised wooden walkways. Visitors can admire views across the dam and Matobo Hills by day, then retire to the tasteful interior of polished wood floors and comfortable wicker furniture. The enormous variety of wildlife makes the Matobo National Park an irresistible location for game drives and bird viewing. Zebra, giraffe, cheetah, rhino and ostrich are just some of species populating what is renowned as one of Zimbabwe's finest sanctuaries. Other activities range from sundowner cruises to fishing, while the more adventurous may wish to explore the spectacular granite Matobo rocks, and discover fine examples of rock art in the caves once inhabited by the bushman. Safaris include visits to the famous 'World's View' where pioneer Cecil Rhodes is buried, and cultural tours to schools, mission stations and the Royal African Village can be arranged. **Directions:** The lodge is 40km from Bulawayo on the eastern boundary of Matobo National Park. Price guide (fully inclusive): Single US$258; Double US$234 per person. Please contact reservations for seasonal specials.

STANLEY & LIVINGSTONE

PO BOX 160, VICTORIA FALLS, ZIMBABWE
TEL: 263 13 4557 HARARE: 263 4 725 797/9 or 263 4 745 011 FAX: 263 13 4421

Named after the two men whose pioneering spirit lives on in the region, this astonishing hotel is under expert management and affords its guests the best of everything. Not only a mere whisper away from the breathtaking falls that Dr David Livingstone discovered and named after Queen Victoria in 1855, the Hotel is a quintessential mixture of opulence and unique hospitality. Unashamedly luxurious, yet relaxed in atmosphere, the thatched complex houses ten spacious suites, each with its own patio, and individually furnished to the highest standard. A warm ambience is created in the main living room and reception area, where timbered ceilings and wooden floors reside tastefully with traditional English décor, and no better a location could be chosen for a small business convention than the elegant, well-equipped boardroom. Gourmet food can be sampled either in the classic dining room, or al fresco on the adjoining elevated patio. Landscaped gardens suddenly end as the real Africa and all its extraordinary wildlife begins. Hotel staff are happy to organise bush meals in the surrounding, natural woodland, as well as visits to The Falls and its various activities. From drinking in the landscape, to wallowing in a gold tapped bath or braving an elephant ride, a visit to The Stanley and Livingstone is an unforgettable adventure. **Directions:** West of Harare, south of Lake Kariba. Price guide (full board): Rooms US$475 per person.

THE VICTORIA FALLS HOTEL

PO BOX 10, VICTORIA FALLS, ZIMBABWE
TEL: 263 13 4751/61 FAX: 263 13 2354/4443 E-MAIL: reservations@tvfh.zimsun.co.zw

Often called the 'grande dame' of Southern Africa's hotels, The Victoria Falls Hotel is an elegant colonial building facing the Victoria Falls Bridge, which traverses the Zambezi River. Originally built of wood under corrugated iron for intrepid tourists, it was completely rebuilt after the first war. Its high ceilings and plush interior are redolent of an age when privilege and a languorous lifestyle were the essence of Colonial life. The Victoria Falls are truly one of the most awe-inspiring sights on earth and the hotel, with its coloured loggias and Renaissance-style balustrades, is the focal point of the majestic scene that greets the visitor. The Victoria Falls Hotel guarantees all of its guests the same regal treatment afforded to the royal families who have visited over nearly a century and assures privacy and indulgence. The many lounges dotted around the hotel offer solitude and calm, while the corridors reflect the empire's past. The Edwardian rooms are beautifully appointed and luxuriously furnished. Afternoon tea is served on the Terrace, which has views over the Falls and the Bridge of unparalleled splendour. Superb dinners are served in the elegant Livingstone Room, which also plays host to ballroom dancing in the evenings. The hotel boasts an Edwardian-style outdoor pool and two floodlit tennis courts. **Directions:** Facing Victoria Falls bridge and spray from the Falls (10 minutes walk). Price guide (incl breakfast): Single US$347–373; double/twin US$193–US$207; suites US$725.

As recommended

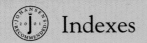

Indexes

Johansens Recommended Hotels Great Britain & Ireland 2001

LONDON

Bloomsbury	The Academy, The Bloomsbury Town House	020 7631 4115
Buckingham Palace	41 Buckingham Palace Road	020 7300 0041
Buckingham Palace	The Rubens at the Palace	020 7834 6600
Chelsea	The Club Suites	020 7730 9131
Chelsea	Draycott House Apartments	020 7584 4659
Chelsea	The Sloane Hotel	020 7581 5757
City	Great Eastern Hotel	020 7618 5000
City	London Bridge Hotel & Apartments	020 7855 2200
City	The Rookery	020 7336 0931
Covent Garden	Kingsway Hall	020 7309 0909
Covent Garden	One Aldwych	020 7300 1000
Hendon	Hendon Hall	020 8203 3341
Holland Park	The Halcyon	020 7727 7288
Kensington	Harrington Hall	020 7396 9696
Kensington	The Lexham Apartments	020 7559 4444
Kensington	The Milestone Hotel	020 7917 1000
Kensington	Twenty Nevern Square	020 7565 9555
Knightsbridge	Basil Street Hotel	020 7581 3311
Knightsbridge	The Beaufort	020 7584 5252
Knightsbridge	Beaufort House Apartments	020 7584 2600
Knightsbridge	The Cadogan	020 7235 7141
Knightsbridge	The Cliveden Town House	020 7730 6466
Knightsbridge	Number Eleven Cadogan Gardens	020 7730 7000
Lancaster Gate	The Hempel	020 7298 9000
Little Venice	The Colonnade The Little Venice Town House	020 7286 1052
Marble Arch	The Leonard	020 7935 2010
Mayfair	The Ascott Mayfair	020 7499 6868
Mayfair	Brown's Hotel	020 7493 6020
Mayfair	The Dorchester	020 7629 8888
Mayfair	Westbury Hotel	020 7629 7755
Notting Hill Gate	Pembridge Court Hotel	020 7229 9977
Richmond Upon Thames	The Petersham Hotel	020 8940 7471
St Pancras	Shaw Park Plaza	020 7666 9000
South Kensington	Number Sixteen	020 7589 5232
Whitehall	The Royal Horseguards	020 7839 3400
Wimbledon Common	Cannizaro House	020 8879 1464

ENGLAND

Aldeburgh	Wentworth Hotel	01728 452312
Alderley Edge	The Alderley Edge Hotel	01625 583033
Alfriston	White Lodge Country House Hotel	01323 870265
Alston	Lovelady Shield Country House Hotel	01434 381203
Altrincham	Woodland Park Hotel	0161 928 8631
Amberley	Amberley Castle	01798 831992
Ambleside	Holbeck Ghyll Country House Hotel	015394 32375
Ambleside	Langdale Hotel & Country Club	015394 37302
Ambleside	Nanny Brow Country House Hotel	015394 32036
Ambleside	Rothay Manor	015394 33605
Andover	Esseborne Manor	01264 736444
Andover	Fifehead Manor	01264 781565
Appleby-in-Westmorland	Appleby Manor Country House Hotel	017683 51571
Appleby-in-Westmorland	Tufton Arms Hotel	017683 51593
Arundel	Bailiffscourt	01903 723511
Ascot	The Berystede	0870 400 8111
Ascot	Pennyhill Park Hotel And Country Club	01276 471774
Ascot	Royal Berkshire	01344 623322
Ashbourne	Callow Hall	01335 300900
Ashbourne	The Izaak Walton Hotel	01335 350555
Ashford	Eastwell Manor	01233 213000

Ashford-In-The-Water	Riverside House	01629 814275
Aylesbury	Hartwell House	01296 747444
Aylesbury	The Priory Hotel	01296 641239
Bakewell	East Lodge Country House Hotel	01629 734474
Bakewell	Hassop Hall	01629 640488
Banbury	Wroxton House Hotel	01295 730777
Barnham Broom	Barnham Broom	01603 759393
Basingstoke	Tylney Hall	01256 764881
Baslow	The Cavendish Hotel	01246 582311
Baslow	Fischer's	01246 583259
Bath	The Bath Priory Hotel and Restaurant	01225 331922
Bath	The Bath Spa Hotel	0870 400 8222
Bath	Combe Grove Manor & Country Club	01225 834644
Bath	Homewood Park	01225 723731
Bath	Hunstrete House	01761 490490
Bath	Lucknam Park	01225 742777
Bath	The Queensberry	01225 447928
Bath	The Royal Crescent Hotel	01225 823333
Bath	Ston Easton Park	01761 241631
Battle	Netherfield Place Hotel & Country Club	01424 774455
Battle	PowderMills Hotel	01424 775511
Beaminster	Bridge House Hotel	01308 862200
Beaulieu	The Master Builder's House	01590 616253
Beaulieu	The Montagu Arms Hotel	01590 612324
Bedford	Woodlands Manor	01234 363281
Berwick-Upon-Tweed	Marshall Meadow Country House Hotel	01289 331133
Berwick-Upon-Tweed	Tillmouth Park	01890 882255
Bibury	The Swan Hotel At Bibury	01285 740695
Birmingham	The Burlington Hotel	0121 643 9191
Birmingham	New Hall	0121 378 2442
Blackburn	Astley Bank Hotel & Conference Centre	01254 777700
Blackpool	The Imperial Hotel	01253 623971
Bolton Abbey	The Devonshire Arms Country House	01756 710441
Bournemouth	The Dormy	01202 872121
Bournemouth	Langtry Manor - Lovenest of a King	01202 553887
Bournemouth	The Norfolk Royale Hotel	01202 551521
Bovey Tracey	The Edgemoor	01626 832466
Box Hill	The Burford Bridge	0870 400 8283
Bradford-On-Avon	Woolley Grange	01225 864705
Brampton	Farlam Hall Hotel	016977 46234
Bray-on-Thames	Chauntry House Hotel & Restaurant	01628 673991
Bray-on-Thames	Monkey Island Hotel	01628 623400
Bristol	Hotel Du Vin & Bistro	0117 925 5577
Bristol	Thornbury Castle	01454 281182
Bristol South	Daneswood House Hotel	01934 843145
Broadway	The Broadway Hotel	01386 852401
Broadway	Buckland Manor Hotel	01386 852626
Broadway	Dormy House	01386 852711
Broadway	The Lygon Arms	01386 852255
Brockenhurst	Careys Manor Hotel	01590 623551
Brockenhurst	New Park Manor	01590 623467
Brockenhurst	Rhinefield House Hotel	01590 622922
Burford	The Bay Tree Hotel & Restaurant	01993 822791
Burnham Market	The Hoste Arms Hotel	01328 738777
Burrington	Northcote Manor Country House Hotel	01769 560501
Bury St Edmunds	The Angel Hotel	01284 714000
Bury St Edmunds	Ravenwood Hall	01359 270345
Buxted	Buxted Park Country House Hotel	01825 732711
Buxton	The Lee Wood Hotel & Restaurant	01298 23002
Canterbury	Howfield Manor	01227 738294
Carne Beach	The Nare Hotel	01872 501111
Castle Combe	The Manor House Hotel & Golf Club	01249 782206
Chaddesley Corbett	Brockencote Hall	01562 777876
Chagford	Gidleigh Park	01647 432367
Chagford	Mill End Hotel	01647 432282
Chelmsford	Pontlands Park Country Hotel	01245 476444

Cheltenham	The Cheltenham Park Hotel	01242 222021
Cheltenham	The Greenway	01242 862352
Cheltenham	Hotel Kandinsky	01242 527788
Cheltenham	Hotel On The Park	01242 518898
Cheltenham	The Queen's	0870 400 8107
Chester	Broxton Hall Country House Hotel	01829 782321
Chester	The Chester Grosvenor	01244 324024
Chester	Crabwall Manor	01244 851666
Chester	Nunsmere Hall	01606 889100
Chester	Rowton Hall Hotel	01244 335262
Chesterfield	Ringwood Hall Hotel	01246 280077
Chichester	The Millstream Hotel	01243 573234
Chipping Campden	Charingworth Manor	01386 593555
Chipping Campden	The Noel Arms Hotel	01386 840111
Chipping Campden	Three Ways Hotel	01386 438429
Chipping Campden	Cotswold House	01386 840330
Cirencester	The Bear of Rodborough Hotel	01453 878522
Clanfield	The Plough at Clanfield	01367 810222
Cobham	Woodlands Park Hotel	01372 843933
Colchester	Five Lakes Hotel Golf Country Club	01621 868888
Coventry	Coombe Abbey	024 76450450
Coventry	Nailcote Hall	024 7646 6174
Crathorne	Crathorne Hall	01642 700398
Crewe	Crewe Hall	01270 253333
Cuckfield	Ockenden Manor	01444 416111
Darlington	Headlam Hall	01325 730238
Dartford	Rowhill Grange Hotel & Spa	01322 615136
Daventry	Fawsley Hall Hotel	01327 892000
Dedham	Maison Talbooth	01206 322367
Durham	Lumley Castle Hotel	0191 389 1111
Eastbourne	The Grand Hotel	01323 412345
Egham	Great Fosters	01784 433822
Evershot	Summer Lodge	01935 83424
Evesham	The Evesham Hotel	01386 765566
Evesham	Wood Norton Hall	01386 420007
Exeter	Combe House at Gittisham	01404 540400
Exeter	Hotel Barcelona	01392 281000
Exeter	The Queens Court Hotel	01392 272709
Exeter	Woodbury Park Hotel	01395 233382
Eye	The Cornwallis Country Hotel	01379 870326
Falmouth	Budock Vean - The Hotel on the River	01326 250288
Falmouth	The Greenbank Hotel	01326 312440
Falmouth	Meudon Hotel	01326 250541
Falmouth	Penmere Manor	01326 211411
Forest Row	Ashdown Park Hotel & Country Club	01342 824988
Fowey	Fowey Hall Hotel & Restaurant	01726 833866
Gatwick	Alexander House	01342 714914
Gatwick	Langshott Manor	01293 786680
Grange-Over-Sands	Graythwaite Manor	015395 32001
Grasmere	Michaels Nook	015394 35496
Grasmere	The Wordsworth Hotel	015394 35592
Guildford	The Angel Posting House And Livery	01483 564555
Guildford	The Manor House	01483 413021
Hadley Wood	West Lodge Park	020 8216 3900
Halifax	Holdsworth House	01422 240024
Hampton Court	The Carlton Mitre Hotel	020 8979 9988
Harrogate	The Balmoral Hotel	01423 508208
Harrogate	The Boar's Head Hotel	01423 771888
Harrogate	Grants Hotel	01423 560666
Harrogate	Hob Green Hotel & Restaurant	01423 770031
Harrogate	Rudding Park House & Hotel	01423 871350
Harwich	The Pier At Harwich	01255 241212
Haslemere	Lythe Hill Hotel	01428 651251
Hathersage	The George at Hathersage	01433 650436
Hawes	Simonstone Hall	01969 667255
Hawkchurch	Fairwater Head Country House Hotel	01297 678349

Location	Hotel	Telephone
Heathrow	Foxhills	01932 704500
Heathrow	Stoke Park Club	01753 717171
Henley-On-Thames	Phyllis Court Club	01491 570500
Hockley Heath	Nuthurst Grange	01564 783972
Horsham	South Lodge Hotel	01403 891711
Hovingham	The Worsley Arms Hotel	01653 628234
Hull	Willerby Manor Hotel	01482 652616
Ilsington	Ilsington Country Hotel	01364 661452
Ipswich	Belstead Brook Hotel	01473 684241
Ipswich	Hintlesham Hall	01473 652268
Ipswich	The Marlborough Hotel	01473 257677
Keswick	The Borrowdale Gates Hotel	017687 77204
Keswick	The Derwentwater Hotel	017687 72538
Kettering	Kettering Park Hotel	01536 416666
Kidderminster	Stone Manor Hotel	01562 777555
King's Lynn	Congham Hall	01485 600250
Kingham	Mill House Hotel	01608 658188
Kingsbridge Estuary	Buckland-Tout-Saints	01548 853055
Knutsford	Mere Court Hotel	01565 831000
Lake Ullswater	Rampsbeck Country House Hotel	017684 86442
Lake Ullswater	Sharrow Bay Country House Hotel	017684 86301
Leamington Spa	Mallory Court	01926 330214
Leeds	42 The Calls	0113 244 0099
Leeds	Haley's Hotel & Restaurant	0113 278 4446
Leeds	Hazlewood Castle Hotel	01937 535353
Leeds	Oulton Hall	0113 282 1000
Leicester	Sketchley Grange Hotel	01455 251133
Lewes	Newick Park	01825 723633
Lichfield	Hoar Cross Hall Health Spa Resort	01283 575671
Lifton	The Arundell Arms	01566 784666
Long Melford	The Black Lion Hotel	01787 312356
Loughborough	Quorn Country Hotel	01509 415050
Louth	Kenwick Park Hotel & Leisure Club	01507 608806
Lower Slaughter	Lower Slaughter Manor	01451 820456
Lower Slaughter	Washbourne Court Hotel	01451 822143
Ludlow	Dinham Hall	01584 876464
Lymington	Passford House Hotel	01590 682398
Lymington	Stanwell House	01590 677123
Lyndhurst	Le Poussin at Parkhill	023 8028 2944
Maidencombe	Orestone Manor Hotel & Restaurant	01803 328098
Maidenhead	Cliveden	01628 668561
Maidenhead	Fredrick's Hotel & Restaurant	01628 581000
Maidenhead	Taplow House Hotel	01628 670056
Maidstone	Chilston Park	01622 859803
Malmesbury	The Old Bell	01666 822344
Malvern	Colwall Park Hotel	01684 540000
Malvern Wells	Cottage In The Wood	01684 575859
Manchester	The Stanneylands Hotel	01625 525225
Manchester Airport	Etrop Grange	0161 499 0500
Marlborough	Ivy House Hotel	01672 515333
Marlow	Compleat Angler	0870 400 8100
Marlow-On-Thames	Danesfield House	01628 891010
Matlock	Riber Hall	01629 582795
Melton Mowbray	Stapleford Park Country House Hotel	01572 787522
Middlecombe	Periton Park Hotel	01643 706885
Midhurst	The Angel Hotel	01730 812421
Midhurst	The Spread Eagle Hotel & Health Spa	01730 816911
Milton Keynes	Moore Place Hotel	01908 282000
Moreton-In-Marsh	The Manor House Hotel	01608 650501
Nantwich	Rookery Hall	01270 610016
Newbury	Donnington Valley Hotel & Golf Club	01635 551199
Newbury	Newbury Manor Hotel	01635 523838
Newbury	The Vineyard At Stockcross	01635 528770
Newcastle-Upon-Tyne	Linden Hall Hotel	01670 50 00 00
Newcastle-Upon-Tyne	Matfen Hall	01661 886 500
Newmarket	Bedford Lodge Hotel	01638 663175
Newmarket	Swynford Paddocks Hotel & Restaurant	01638 570234
Northampton	Whittlebury Hall	01327 857 857
Norwich	Park Farm Hotel & Leisure	01603 810264
Norwich	Petersfield House Hotel	01692 630741
Nottingham	Langar Hall	01949 860559
Oakham	Hambleton Hall	01572 756991
Otley	Chevin Lodge Country Park Hotel	01943 467818
Oxford	The Cotswold Lodge Hotel	01865 512121
Oxford	Fallowfields	01865 820416
Oxford	Le Manoir aux Quat' Saisons	01844 278881
Oxford	The Randolph	0870 400 8200
Oxford	Studley Priory	01865 351203
Oxford	Weston Manor	01869 350621
Padstow	Treglos Hotel	01841 520727
Painswick	The Painswick Hotel	01452 812160
Peterborough	The Haycock	01780 782223
Plymouth	Kitley House Hotel & Restaurant	01752 881555
Polperro	Talland Bay Hotel	01503 272667
Prestbury	The Bridge Hotel	01625 829326
Preston	The Gibbon Bridge Country House Hotel	01995 61456
Redhill	Nutfield Priory	01737 824400
Richmond-Upon-Thames	The Richmond Gate Hotel	020 8940 0061
Risley	Risley Hall Country House Hotel	0115 939 9000
Ross-On-Wye	The Chase Hotel	01989 763161
Ross-On-Wye	Pengethley Manor	01989 730211
Rusper	Ghyll Manor Country Hotel	01293 871571
Rutland Water	Barnsdale Lodge	01572 724678
St Agnes	Rose-in-Vale Country House Hotel	01872 552202
St Albans	Sopwell House Hotel Country Club	01727 864477
St Albans	The St Michael's Manor	01727 864444
St. Ives	The Garrack Hotel & Restaurant	01736 796199
St Keyne	The Well House	01579 342001
St.Mawes	The Rosevine Hotel	01872 580206
Salcombe	Bolt Head Hotel	01548 843751
Salcombe	Soar Mill Cove Hotel	01548 561566
Salcombe	The Tides Reach Hotel	01548 843466
Salisbury	Howard's House	01722 716392
Scarborough	Hackness Grange	01723 882345
Scarborough	Wrea Head Country Hotel	01723 378211
Seaview	The Priory Bay Hotel	01983 613146
Sheffield	Charnwood Hotel	0114 258 9411
Sheffield	Whitley Hall Hotel	0114 245 4444
Shepton Mallet	Charlton House & Mulberry Restaurant	01749 342008
Shrewsbury	Prince Rupert Hotel	01743 499955
Sidmouth	Hotel Riviera	01395 515201
Sonning-On-Thames	The French Horn	01189 692204
Southwold	The Swan Hotel	01502 722186
Stafford	The Moat House	01785 712217
Stamford	The George Of Stamford	01780 750750
Stansted	Down Hall Country House Hotel	01279 731441
Stansted	Whitehall	01279 850603
Stow-On-The-Wold	The Grapevine Hotel	01451 830344
Stow-On-The-Wold	Lords Of The Manor Hotel	01451 820243
Stow-On-The-Wold	The Unicorn Hotel	01451 830257
Stow-On-The-Wold	Wyck Hill House	01451 831936
Stratford-Upon-Avon	Alveston Manor	0870 400 1818
Stratford-Upon-Avon	Ettington Park	01789 450123
Stratford-Upon-Avon	Salford Hall Hotel	01386 871300
Stratford-Upon-Avon	Welcombe Hotel & Golf Course	01789 295252
Streatley-On-Thames	The Swan Diplomat Hotel	01491 873737
Sturminster Newton	Plumber Manor	01258 472507
Swindon	The Pear Tree at Purton	01793 772100
Taunton	Bindon Country House Hotel	01823 400070
Taunton	The Mount Somerset Hotel	01823 442500
Telford	Madeley Court	01952 680068
Tetbury	Calcot Manor	01666 890391
Teukesbury	Corse Lawn House Hotel	01452 780479
Thame	The Spread Eagle Hotel	01844 213661
Thetford	Lynford Hall Hotel & Business Centre	01842 878351
Thirsk	Crab Manor	01845 577286
Ticehurst	Dale Hill	01580 200112
Torquay	The Osborne Hotel & Langtry's	01803 213311
Torquay	The Palace Hotel	01803 200200
Tring	Pendley Manor Hotel	01442 891891
Tunbridge Wells	Hotel Du Vin & Bistro	01892 526455
Tunbridge Wells	The Spa Hotel	01892 520331
Uppingham	The Lake Isle	01572 822951
Ware	Hanbury Manor	01920 487722
Wareham	The Priory	01929 551666
Warminster	Bishopstrow House	01985 212312
Warwick	The Glebe At Barford	01926 624218
Wells	The Market Place Hotel	01749 672616
Wetherby	Wood Hall	01937 587271
Weybridge	Oatlands Park Hotel	01932 847242
Weymouth	Moonfleet Manor	01305 786948
Wincanton	Holbrook House Hotel	01963 32377
Winchester	Hotel Du Vin & Bistro	01962 841414
Winchester	Lainston House Hotel	01962 863588
Windermere	Gilpin Lodge	015394 88818
Windermere	Lakeside Hotel On Lake Windermere	0541 541586
Windermere	Langdale Chase	015394 32201
Windermere	Linthwaite House Hotel	015394 88600
Windermere	Miller Howe	015394 42536
Windermere	Storrs Hall	015394 47111
Windsor	The Castle Hotel	0870 400 8300
Windsor	Sir Christopher Wren's Hotel	01753 861354
Woburn	The Bedford Arms	01525 290441
Woburn	Flitwick Manor	01525 712242
Wolverhampton	The Old Vicarage Hotel	01746 716497
Woodbridge	Seckford Hall	01394 385678
Woodstock	The Feathers Hotel	01993 812291
Woolacombe	Watersmeet Hotel	01271 870333
Woolacombe	Woolacombe Bay Hotel	01271 870388
Worcester	The Elms	01299 896666
Yarmouth I.O.W	The George Hotel	01983 760331
York	Ambassador Hotel	01904 641316
York	The Grange Hotel	01904 644744
York	Middlethorpe Hall	01904 641241
York	Monk Fryston Hall Hotel	01977 682369
York	Mount Royale Hotel	01904 628856

IRELAND

Belfast	Culloden Hotel	028 9042 5223
Belfast	The McCausland Hotel	028 9022 0200
Carrickmacross	Nuremore Hotel & Country Club	00 353 429 661438
Clonakilty	The Lodge & Spa at Inchydoney Island	00 353 23 33143
Cong	Ashford Castle	00 353 92 46003
Connemara	Renvyle House Hotel	00 353 95 43511
Cork	Hayfield Manor Hotel	00 353 21 4315600
Dublin	Brooks Hotel	00 353 1 670 4000
Dublin	The Davenport Hotel	00 353 1 607 3500
Dublin	The Fitzwilliam Hotel	00 353 1 478 7000
Dublin	The Hibernian	00 353 1 668 7666
Dublin	Kildare Hotel & Country Club	00 353 1 601 7200
Dublin	The Merrion Hotel	00 353 1 603 0600
Dublin	Stephen's Green Hotel	00 353 1 607 3600
Ennis	Woodstock Hotel	00 353 65 684 6600
Galway	Connemara Coast Hotel	00 353 91 592108
Gorey	Marlfield House	00 353 55 21124
Kenmare	The Park Hotel Kenmare	00 353 64 41200
Kenmare	Sheen Falls Lodge	00 353 64 41600
Kilkenny	Kilkenny Ormonde Hotel	00 353 56 23900
Killarney	Aghadoe Heights Hotel	00 353 64 31766
Killarney	The Killarney Park Hotel	00 353 64 35555
Mallow	Longueville House	00 353 22 47156
Newmarket-On-Fergus	Dromoland Castle	00 353 61 368144
Parknasilla	Parknasilla Hotel	00 353 64 45122
Rathnew	Hunter's Hotel	00 353 404 40106
Rosslare	Kelly's Resort Hotel	00 353 53 32114
Rossnowlagh	The Sand House Hotel	00 353 72 51777
Westport	Knockranny House Hotel	00 353 98 28600
Wicklow	Tinakilly Country House Hotel	00 353 40469274

SCOTLAND

Aberdeen	Ardoe House Hotel & Restaurant	01224 860600
Aberdeen	Thainstone House Hotel & Country Club	01467 621643
Aberfoyle	Forest Hills	01877 387277
Auchencairn	Balcary Bay Hotel	01556 640311
Auchterarder	Auchterarder House	01764 663646
Ballantrae	Glenapp Castle	01465 831212
Ballater	Darroch Learg Hotel	013397 55443
Banchory	Raemoir House Hotel	01330 824884
Beasdale By Arisaig	Arisaig House	01687 450622
Biggar	Shieldhill Castle	01899 220035
Blairgowrie	Kinloch House Hotel	01250 884237
Craigellachie	Craigellachie Hotel	01340 881204
Dunkeld	Kinnaird	01796 482 440
Dunoon	Enmore Hotel	01369 702230
East Kilbride	Macdonald Crutherland House Hotel	01355 577000
Edinburgh	The Bonham	0131 226 6050
Edinburgh	Borthwick Castle	01875 820514
Edinburgh	Channings	0131 315 2226
Edinburgh	Dalhousie Castle & Spa	01875 820153
Edinburgh	The Howard	0131 557 3500
Edinburgh	The Norton House Hotel	0131 333 1275
Edinburgh	Prestonfield House	0131 668 3346
Edinburgh	The Roxburgh	0131 240 5500
Edinburgh	The Scotsman	0131 556 5565
Elgin	Mansion House Hotel	01343 548811
Gatehouse Of Fleet	Cally Palace Hotel	01557 814341
Glasgow	Carlton George Hotel	0141 353 6373
Glasgow	Gleddoch House	01475 540711
Glenshee	Dalmunzie House	01250 885224
Grantown-On-Spey	Muckrach Lodge Hotel & Restaurant	01479 851257
Inverness	Bunchrew House Hotel	01463 234917
Inverness	Culloden House Hotel	01463 790461
Kelso	Ednam House Hotel	01573 224168
Kelso	The Roxburghe Hotel & Golf Course	01573 450331
Kilchrenan by Oban	Ardanaiseig	01866 833333
Kildrummy	Kildrummy Castle Hotel	019755 71288
Kinbuck	Cromlix House	01786 822125
Lochinver	Inver Lodge Hotel	01571 844496
Lockerbie	The Dryfesdale Country House Hotel	01576 202427
Newton Stewart	Kirroughtree House	01671 402141
Oban	Knipoch Hotel	01852 316251
Peebles	Cringletie House Hotel	01721 730233
Perth	Ballathie House Hotel	01250 883268
Perth	Huntingtower Hotel	01738 583771
Perth	Kinfauns Castle	01738 620777
Pitlochry	Pine Trees Hotel	01796 472121
Portpatrick	Fernhill Hotel	01776 810220
St Andrews	The Inn at Lathones	01334 840 494
St Boswells	Dryburgh Abbey Hotel	01835 822261
Stirling	Stirling Highland Hotel	01786 272727
Stranraer	Corsewall Lighthouse Hotel	01776 853220
Torridon	Loch Torridon Hotel	01445 791242
Troon	Lochgreen House	01292 313343
Troon	Piersland House Hotel	01292 314747
Uphall	Houstoun House	01506 853831

WALES

Aberdare	Ty Newydd Country Hotel	01685 813433
Abergavenny	Allt-Yr-Ynys Hotel	01873 890307
Abergavenny	Llansantffraed Court Hotel	01873 840678
Abersoch	Porth Tocyn Country House Hotel	01758 713303
Aberystwyth	Conrah Country House Hotel	01970 617941
Anglesey	Trearddur Bay Hotel	01407 860301
Bala	Palé Hall	01678 530285
Barmouth	Bontddu Hall	01341 430661
Beaumaris	Ye Olde Bull's Head	01248 810329
Brecon	Llangoed Hall	01874 754525
Brecon	Peterstone Court	01874 665387
Brecon Beacons	Nant Ddu Lodge Hotel	01685 379111
Cardiff	Miskin Manor Country House Hotel	01443 224204
Corwen	Tyddyn Llan Country House Hotel	01490 440264
Crickhowell	Gliffaes Country House Hotel	01874 730371
Dolgellau	Penmaenuchaf Hall	01341 422129
Harlech	Hotel Maes-Y-Neuadd	01766 780200
Lake Vyrnwy	Lake Vyrnwy Hotel	01691 870 692
Llandudno	Bodysgallen Hall	01492 584466
Llandudno	St Tudno Hotel	01492 874411
Llangammarch Wells	The Lake Country House	01591 620202
Machynlleth	Ynyshir Hall	01654 781209
Pembroke	The Court Hotel & Restaurant	01646 672273
Portmeirion Village	The Portmeirion and Castell Deudraeth	01766 770000
St David's	Warpool Court Hotel	01437 720300
Tenby	Penally Abbey	01834 843033
Usk	The Cwrt Bleddyn Hotel	01633 450521
Wrexham	Llyndir Hall Hotel	01244 571648

CHANNEL ISLANDS

Guernsey	Old Government House Hotel	01481 724921
Guernsey	St Pierre Park Hotel	01481 728282
Jersey	The Atlantic Hotel	01534 744101
Jersey	Château La Chaire	01534 863354
Jersey	Hotel L'Horizon	01534 743101
Jersey	Longueville Manor	01534 725501

Johansens Recommended Traditional Inns, Hotels & Restaurants 2001

ENGLAND

Ashbourne	Red Lion Inn	01335 370396
Ashbourne/Uttoxeter	Beeches Restaurant	01889 590288
Bakewell	The Peacock Hotel at Rowsley	01629 733518
Belford	The Blue Bell Hotel	01668 213543
Brancaster Staithe	The White Horse	01485 210262
Bridport	The Manor Hotel	01308 897616
Brighton	The Old Tollgate Restaurant And Hotel	01903 879494
Burford	The Lamb Inn	01993 823155
Burnsall	The Red Lion	01756 720204
Burton Upon Trent	Boar's Head Hotel	01283 820344
Burton upon Trent	Ye Olde Dog & Partridge	01283 813030
Calver	The Chequers Inn	01433 630231
Camborne	Tyacks Hotel	01209 612424
Cambridge	The White Horse Inn	01440 706081
Carlisle	The Tarn End House Hotel	016977 2340
Chesterfield / Sheffield	Manor House Hotel & Restaurant	01246 413971
Christchurch	The Lord Bute	01425 278884
Cirencester	The New Inn at Coln	01285 750651
Clare	The Plough Inn	01440 786789
Clavering	The Cricketers	01799 550442
Coleford	The New Inn	01363 84242
Compton Bassett	White Horse Inn	01249 813118
Coningsby	The Lea Gate Inn	01526 342370
Cranbrook	The George Hotel	01580 713348
Ditcheat	The Manor House Inn	01749 860276
Dorchester-On-Thames	The George Hotel	01865 340404
East Witton	The Blue Lion	01969 624273
Egton	The Wheatsheaf Inn	01947 895271
Eton	The Christopher Hotel	01753 811677
Evershot	Acorn Inn	01935 83228
Evesham	Riverside Restaurant And Hotel	01386 446200
Exmoor	The Royal Oak Inn	01643 851455
Falmouth	Trengilly Wartha Country Inn	01326 340332
Fordingbridge	The Three Lions Restaurant	01425 652489
Goring-On-Thames	The Leatherne Bottel Riverside Inn	01491 872667
Grimsthorpe	The Black Horse Inn	01778 591247
Grindleford	The Maynard Arms	01433 630321
Halifax/Huddersfield	The Rock Inn Hotel	01422 379721
Handcross	The Chequers At Slaugham	01444 400239
Harrogate	The Boar's Head Hotel	01423 771888
Harrogate	The George	01765 677214
Hathersage	The Plough Inn	01433 650319
Hayfield	The Waltzing Weasel	01663 743402
Helmsley	The Feathers Hotel	01439 770275
Helmsley	The Feversham Arms Hotel	01439 770766
Hindon	The Grosvenor Arms	01747 820696
Holt	The Roman Camp Inn	01263 838291
Honiton	Home Farm Hotel	01404 831278
Huddersfield	The Weavers Shed Restaurant with Rooms	01484 654284
Kenilworth	Clarendon House Bar Brasserie Hotel	01926 857668
Knutsford	Longview Hotel And Restaurant	01565 632119
Leek	The Three Horseshoes Inn & Kirk's	01538 300296
Longleat	The Bath Arms	01985 844308
Lymington	Gordleton Mill Inn	01590 682219
Lynmouth	The Rising Sun	01598 753223
Maidstone	Ringlestone Inn and Farmhouse Hotel	01622 859900
Malmesbury	The Horse And Groom Inn	01666 823904
Mells	The Talbot Inn at Mells	01373 812254
Mildenhall	The Bell Hotel	01638 717272
Newby Bridge	The Swan Hotel	015395 31681
Nottingham	Hotel Des Clos	01159 866566
Oxford	Holcombe Hotel	01869 338274
Oxford	The Jersey Arms	01869 343234
Padstow	The Old Custom House Hotel	01841 532359
Pangbourne	The George Hotel	01189 842237
Pelynt	Jubilee Inn	01503 220312
Penzance	The Summer House	01736 363744
Pickering	The White Swan	01751 472288
Port Gaverne	The Port Gaverne Inn	01208 880244
Preston	Ye Horn's Inn	01772 865230
Rugby	The Golden Lion Inn of Easenhall	01788 832265
Saddleworth	The Old Bell Inn Hotel	01457 870130
Shipton Under Wychwood	The Shaven Crown Hotel	01993 830330
Snettisham	The Rose & Crown	01485 541382
Stamford	Black Bull Inn	01476 860086
Stamford	The Crown Hotel	01780 763136
Stanton Wick	The Carpenters Arms	01761 490202
Stow-On-The-Wold	The Kings Head Inn & Restaurant	01608 658365
Telford	The Hundred House Hotel	01952 730353
Thaxted	Recorders House Restaurant	01371 830438
Thirsk	Crab & Lobster	01845 577286
Thornham	The Lifeboat Inn	01485 512236
Thorpe Market	Green Farm Restaurant And Hotel	01263 833602
Tintagel	The Port William	01840 770230
Totnes	The Sea Trout Inn	01803 762274
Upton-Upon-Severn	The White Lion Hotel	01684 592551
West Auckland	The Manor House Hotel & Country Club	01388 834834
Whitewell	The Inn At Whitewell	01200 448222
Wisbech	Crown Lodge Hotel	01945 773391
Wooler	The Tankerville Arms Hotel	01668 281581

SCOTLAND

Annan	The Powfoot Hotel	01461 700254
Edinburgh	Bank Hotel	0131 556 9940
Isle Of Skye	Hotel Eilean Iarmain	01471 833332
Kylesku	Kylesku Hotel	01971 502231
Loch Earn	Achray House on Loch Earn	01764 685231
Moffat	Annandale Arms Hotel	01683 220013
Oldmeldrum	The Redgarth	01651 872 353
Plockton	The Plockton Hotel & Garden Restaurant	01599 544274
Poolewe	Pool House Hotel	01445 781272
Stirling	Sheriffmuir Inn	01786 823285
Tighnabruaich	Royal Hotel	01700 811239

WALES

Bridgend	The Great House	01656 657644
Llanarmon Dyffryn Ceiriog	The West Arms Hotel	01691 600665
Presteigne	The Radnorshire Arms	01544 267406

CHANNEL ISLANDS

Guernsey	Les Rocquettes Hotel	01481 722176

ENGLAND

Albrighton	The Grange Hotel	01902 701711
Alcester	Arrow Mill Hotel And Restaurant	01789 762419
Alcester	The Old Windmill	01386 792801
Ambleside	Nanny Brow Country House Hotel	015394 32036
Ampleforth	Shallowdale House	01439 788325
Appleton-Le-Moors	Appleton Hall	01751 417227
Arundel	Burpham Country House Hotel	01903 882160
Ashington	The Mill House Hotel	01903 892426
Atherstone	Chapel House	01827 718949
Bamburgh	Waren House Hotel	01668 214581
Barnstaple	Downrew House Hotel	01271 342497
Bath	Apsley House	01225 336966
Bath	Bath Lodge Hotel	01225 723040
Bath	The County Hotel	01225 425003
Bath	The Old Priory Hotel	01761 416784
Bath	Paradise House	01225 317723
Bath	Villa Magdala	01225 466329
Bath	Widbrook Grange	01225 864750
Bath	Woolverton House	01373 830415
Beccles	The Elms	01502 677380
Bibury	Bibury Court	01285 740337
Biggin-By-Hartington	Biggin Hall	01298 84451
Billericay	The Pump House Apartment	01277 656579
Blockley	Lower Brook House	01386 700286
Bourton-On-The-Water	Dial House Hotel	01451 822244
Brighton	The Granville	01273 326302
Brockenhurst	Thatched Cottage Hotel & Restaurant	01590 623090
Brockenhurst	Whitley Ridge & Country House Hotel	01590 622354
Bromsgrove	Grafton Manor Country House Hotel	01527 579007
Cambridge	Melbourn Bury	01763 261151
Carlisle	Crosby Lodge Country House Hotel	01228 573618
Cartmel	Aynsome Manor Hotel	015395 36653
Cheddar	Daneswood House Hotel	01934 843145
Cheltenham	Charlton Kings Hotel	01242 231061
Chester	Green Bough Hotel	01244 326241
Chichester	Crouchers Bottom Country Hotel	01243 784995
Chippenham	Stanton Manor	01666 837552
Chipping Campden	The Malt House	01386 840295
Clearwell	Tudor Farmhouse Hotel & Restaurant	01594 833046
Coalville	Abbots Oak	01530 832 328
Combe Martin	Ashelford	01271 850469
Crediton	Coombe House Country Hotel	01363 84487
Dartmoor	Bel Alp House	01364 661217
Derby	The Homestead	01332 544300
Diss	Chippenhall Hall	01379 588180
Dorchester	Yalbury Cottage Hotel	01305 262382
Dorchester-On-Thames	The George Hotel	01865 340404
Dover	Wallett's Court	01304 852424
Dulverton	Ashwick Country House Hotel	01398 323868
Enfield	Oak Lodge Hotel	020 8360 7082
Epsom	Chalk Lane Hotel	01372 721179
Falmouth	Trelawne Hotel-The Hutches Restaurant	01326 250226
Folkestone	Sandgate Hotel at Restaurant La Terrasse	01303 220444
Gatwick	Stanhill Court Hotel	01293 862166
Glossop	The Wind In The Willows	01457 868001
Golant by Fowey	The Cormorant Hotel	01726 833426`
Grasmere	White Moss House	015394 35295
Great Snoring	The Old Rectory	01328 820597
Hadleigh	'Edge Hall' Hotel	01473 822458
Hampton Court	Chase Lodge	020 8943 1862
Hamsterley Forest	Grove House	01388 488203
Harrogate	The White House	01423 501388
Hawes	Rookhurst Country House Hotel	01969 667454
Hawkshead	Sawrey House Country Hotel	015394 36387
Helmsley	The Pheasant	01439 771241
Helston	Nansloe Manor	01326 574691
Hereford	The Steppes	01432 820424
Higham	Santo's Higham Farm	01773 833812
Holt	Felbrigg Lodge	01263 837588
Ilminster	The Old Rectory	01460 54364
Ilsington	Ilsington Country Hotel	01364 661452
Isle of Wight	Rylstone Manor	01983 862806
Keswick	Dale Head Hall Lakeside Hotel	017687 72478
Keswick	Swinside Lodge Hotel	017687 72948
Kingsbridge	The White House	01548 580580
Kirkby Lonsdale	Hipping Hall	015242 71187
Launceston	Penhallow Manor Country House Hotel	01566 86206
Leominster	Lower Bache House	01568 750304
Lincoln	Washingborough Hall	01522 790340
Lorton	Winder Hall	01900 85107
Loughborough	The Old Manor Hotel	01509 211228
Ludlow	Overton Grange Hotel	01584 873500
Luton	Little Offley	01462 768243
Lydford	Moor View House	01822 820220
Lymington	The Nurse's Cottage	01590 683402
Manchester	Eleven Didsbury Park	0161 448 7711
Membury	Oxenways	01404 881785
Middlecombe	Periton Park Hotel	01643 706885
Middleham	Waterford House	01969 622090
Minchinhampton	Burleigh Court	01453 883804
Morchard Bishop	Wigham	01363 877350
New Romney	Romney Bay House	01797 364747
Newent	Three Choirs	01531 890223
North Bovey	Blackaller	01647 440322
North Norfolk Coast	The Great Escape Holiday Company	01485 518717
North Walsham	Beechwood Hotel	01692 403231
North Walsham	Elderton Lodge	01263 833547
Norwich	The Beeches Hotel & Victorian Gardens	01603 621167
Norwich	Catton Old Hall	01603 419379
Norwich	Norfolk Mead Hotel	01603 737531
Norwich	The Old Rectory	01603 700772
Norwich	The Stower Grange	01603 860210
Nottingham	Cockliffe Country House Hotel	01159 680179
Nottingham	The Cottage Country House Hotel	01159 846882
Nottingham	Langar Hall	01949 860559
Nottingham	Sutton Bonnington Hall	01509 672355
Ockham	The Hautboy	01483 225355
Oswestry	Pen-y-Dyffryn Country Hotel	01691 653700
Otterburn	The Otterburn Tower	01830 520620
Overstrand	Sea Marge Hotel	01263 579579
Owlpen	Owlpen Manor	01453 860261
Oxford	Fallowfields	01865 820416
Oxford	Westwood Country House	01865 735408
Padstow	Cross House Hotel	01841 532391
Penrith	Temple Sowerby House Hotel	017683 61578
Petersfield	Langrish House	01730 266941
Porlock Weir	Andrew's On The Weir	01643 863300
Porthleven	Tye Rock Country House & Apartments	01326 572695
Portsmouth	The Beaufort Hotel	023 92823707
Pulborough	Chequers Hotel	01798 872486
Ringwood	Moortown Lodge	01425 471404
Ross-On-Wye	Glewstone Court	01989 770367
Ross-On-Wye	Wilton Court Hotel	01989 562569
Rye	White Vine House	01797 224748
St Ives	The Countryman At Trink Hotel	01736 797571
St Keyne	The Old Rectory Country House Hotel	01579 342617
St Mawes	The Hundred House Hotel	01872 501336
Saunton	Preston House Hotel	01271 890472
Sherborne	The Grange Hotel & Restaurant	01935 813463
Shipton Under Wychwood	The Shaven Crown Hotel	01993 830330
Shrewsbury	Rowton Castle Hotel	01743 884044
Shrewsbury	Upper Brompton Farm	01743 761629
Southport	Tree Tops Country House Restaurant	01704 572430
Stanhope	Horsley Hall	01388 517239
Staverton	Kingston House	01803 762 235
Stevenage	Redcoats Farmhouse Hotel & Restaurant	01438 729500
Stow-On-The-Wold	The Tollgate Inn	01608 658389
Stratford-upon-Avon	Glebe Farm House	01789 842501
Tarporley	Willington Hall Hotel	01829 752321
Tavistock	Browns Hotel Wine bar & Brasserie	01822 618686
Thetford	Broom Hall Country Hotel	01953 882125
Tintagel	Trebrea Lodge	01840 770410
Uckfield	Hooke Hall	01825 761578
Wadebridge	Tredethy House	01208 841262
Wadebridge	Trehellas House & Memories of Malaya Restaurant	01208 72700
Warwick	The Ardencote Manor Hotel	01926 843111
Wells	Beryl	01749 678738
Wells	Glencot House	01749 677160
Wem	Soulton Hall	01939 232786
Wimborne Minster	Beechleas	01202 841684
Windermere	Broadoaks Country House	01539 445566
Windermere	Fayrer Garden House Hotel	015394 88195
Windermere	Lakeshore House	015394 33202
Witherslack	The Old Vicarage Country House Hotel	015395 52381
York	The Parsonage Country House Hotel	01904 728111

IRELAND

Caragh Lake Co Kerry	Caragh Lodge	00 353 66 9769115
Cashel Co Tipperary	Cashel Palace Hotel	00 353 62 62707
Connemara	Ross Lake House Hotel	00 353 91 550109
Craughwell	St. Clerans	00 353 91 846 555
Killarney	Killarney Royal Hotel	00 353 64 31853
Killarney Co Kerry	Earls Court House	00 353 64 34009
Kilmeaden	The Old Rectory - Kilmeaden House	00 353 51 384254
Letterkenny	Castle Grove Country House Hotel	00 353 745 1118
Riverstown,Co Sligo	Coopershill House	00 353 71 65108
Sligo,Co Sligo	Markree Castle	00 353 71 67800

SCOTLAND

Ballater,Royal Deeside	Balgonie Country House	013397 55482
Banchory	Banchory Lodge Hotel	01330 822625
Cornhill	Castle of Park	01466 751111
Dunfries	Trigony House Hotel	01848 331211
Dunkeld	The Pend	01350 727586
Edinburgh	Garvock House Hotel	01383 621067
Fintry	Culcreuch Castle Hotel & Country Park	01360 860555
Glen Cannich	Mullardoch House Hotel	01456 415460
Inverness	Culduthel Lodge	01463 240089
Isle Of Harris	Ardvourlie Castle	01859 502307
Kentallen Of Appin	Ardsheal House	01631 740227
Killiecrankie,By Pitlochry	The Killiecrankie Hotel	01796 473220
Leslie	Balgeddie House Hotel	01592 742511
Maybole	Culzean Castle	01655 884455
Nairn	Boath House	01667 454896
Oban	Dungallan House Hotel	01631 563799
Pitlochry	Knockendarroch House	01796 473473
Port Of Menteith	The Lake Hotel	01877 385258
Rothiemurchus	Corrour House	01479 810220
St. Andrews	The Inn on North Steet	01334 473387
St Fillans	The Four Seasons Hotel	01764 685333
Tain	Glenmorangie House at Cadbol	01862 871671

WALES

Aberdovey	Plas Penhelig Country House Hotel	01654 767676
Betws-y-Coed	Tan-y-Foel	01690 710507
Caernarfon	Ty'n Rhos Country Hotel	01248 670489
Cardiff	Llechwen Hall	01443 742050
Conwy	The Old Rectory Country House	01492 580611
Criccieth	Tyddyn Iolyn	01766 522509
Dolgellau	Abergwynant Hall	01341 422160
Dolgellau	Plas Dolmelynllyn	01341 440273
Llandeilo	The Cawdor Arms Hotel	01558 823500
Monmouth	The Crown At Whitebrook	01600 860254
Swansea	Norton House Hotel & Restaurant	01792 404891
Tenby	Waterwynch House Hotel	01834 842464
Tintern	Parva Farmhouse and Restaurant	01291 689411

CHANNEL ISLANDS

Guernsey	Bella Luce Hotel & Restaurant	01481 238764
Guernsey	La Favorita Hotel	01481 35666
Herm Island	The White House	01481 722159
Sark Island	La Sablonnerie	01481 832061

MINI LISTINGS
Johansens Recommended Hotels – Europe & The Mediterranean 2001
Here in brief are the entries that appear in full in Johansens Recommended Hotels – Europe & The Mediterranean 2001.
To order Johansens guides turn to the order forms at the back of this book.

AUSTRIA/CARINTHIA (KLAGENFURT)
Hotel Palais Porcia
Neuer Platz 13, 9020 Klagenfurt, Austria
Tel: 43 463 51 15 90
Fax: 43 463 51 15 90 30

AUSTRIA/CARINTHIA (PATERGASSEN)
Almdorf "Seinerzeit"
Fellacher alm, 9564 Patergassen
Kleinkirchheim, Austria
Tel: 43 4275 7201
Fax: 43 4275 7380

AUSTRIA/CARINTHIA (VELDEN)
Seeschlössl Velden
Klagenfurter Strasse 34, 9220 Velden,
Austria
Tel: 43 4274 2824
Fax: 43 4274 282444

AUSTRIA/LOWER AUSTRIA (DÜRNSTEIN)
Hotel Schloss Dürnstein
3601 Dürnstein, Austria
Tel: 43 2711 212
Fax: 43 2711 351

AUSTRIA/SALZBURG (BAD GASTEIN)
Hotel & Spa Haus Hirt
Kaiserhofstrasse 14, 5640 Bad Gastein,
Austria
Tel: 43 64 34 27 97
Fax: 43 64 34 27 97 48

AUSTRIA/SALZBURG (BAD HOFGASTEIN)
Das Moser
Kaiser-Franz-Platz 2, 5630 Bad Hofgastein,
Austria
Tel: 43 6432 6209
Fax: 43 6432 6209 88

AUSTRIA/SALZBURG (SALZBURG)
Hotel Auersperg
Auerspergstrasse 61, 5027 Salzburg, Austria
Tel: 43 662 88 944
Fax: 43 662 88 944 55

AUSTRIA/SALZBURG (SALZBURG)
Hotel Schloss Mönchstein
Mönchsberg Park, City Center 26, 5020
Salzburg, Austria
Tel: 43 662 84 85 55 0
Fax: 43 662 84 85 59

AUSTRIA/STYRIA (GRAZ)
Schlossberg Hotel
Kaiser-Franz-Josef-Kai 30, 8010 Graz,
Austria
Tel: 43 316 80700
Fax: 43 316 807070

AUSTRIA/TYROL (ALPBACH)
Romantik Hotel Böglerhof
6236 Aplbach Austria
Tel: 43 5336 5227
Fax: 43 5336 5227 402

AUSTRIA/TYROL (IGLS)
Schlosshotel Igls
Viller Steig 2, 6080 Igls, Austria
Tel: 43 512 37 72 17
Fax: 43 512 37 86 79

AUSTRIA/TYROL (IGLS)
Sporthotel Igls
Hilberstrasse 17, 6080 Igls, Austria
Tel: 43 512 37 72 41
Fax: 43 512 37 86 79

AUSTRIA/TYROL (INNSBRUCK)
Romantik Hotel Schwarzer Adler
Kaiserjägerstrasse 2, 6020 Innsbruck, Austria
Tel: 43 512 587109
Fax: 43 512 561697

AUSTRIA/TYROL (KITZBÜHEL)
Romantik Hotel Tennerhof
Griesenauweg 26, 6370 Kitzbühel, Austria
Tel: 43 53566 3181
Fax: 43 53566 318170

AUSTRIA/TYROL (SANKT CHRISTOPH)
Arlberg Hospiz
6580 St Christoph, Austria
Tel: 43 5446 2611
Fax: 43 5446 3545

AUSTRIA/TYROL (SEEFELD)
Hotel Klosterbräu
Am Sonnenplatz 1, 6100 Seefeld, Austria
Tel: 43 521 226210
Fax: 43 521 223885

AUSTRIA/UPPER AUSTRIA (GRÜNAU)
Romantik Hotel Almtalhof
4645 Grünau Im Almtal, Austria
Tel: 43 7616 82040
Fax: 43 7616 820466

AUSTRIA/UPPER AUSTRIA (ST WOLFGANG AM SEE)
Romantik Hotel im Weissen Rössl
5360 St Wolfgang am See, Salzkammergut,
Austria
Tel: 43 6138 23060
Fax: 43 6138 2306 41

AUSTRIA/VIENNA (VIENNA)
Ana Grand Hotel Wien
Kärntner Ring 9, 1010 Vienna, Austria
Tel: 43 1 515 80721
Fax: 43 1 515 1310

AUSTRIA/VIENNA (VIENNA)
Hotel im Palais Schwarzenberg
Schwarzenbergplatz 9, 1030 Vienna, Austria
Tel: 43 1 798 4515
Fax: 43 1 798 4714

AUSTRIA/VORARLBERG (BEZAU)
Hotel Gasthof Gams
6870 Bezau, Austria
Tel: 43 5514 2220
Fax: 43 5514 222 024

AUSTRIA/VORARLBERG (LECH)
Sporthotel Kristiania
Omesberg 331, 6764 Lech am Arlberg,
Austria
Tel: 43 55 83 25 610
Fax: 43 55 83 35 50

AUSTRIA/VORARLBERG (LECH)
Hotel Goldener Berg
Po Box 33, 6764 Lech am Arlberg, Austria
Tel: 43 5583 22050
Fax: 43 5583 220513

AUSTRIA/VORARLBERG (SCHWARZENBERG IM BREGENZERWALD)
Romantik Hotel Gasthof Hirschen
Hof 14, 6867 Schwarzenberg, Austria
Tel: 43 5512 29 44 0
Fax: 43 5512 29 44 20

AUSTRIA/VORARLBERG (ZÜRS)
Thurnhers Alpenhof
6763 Zürs am Arlberg, Austria
Tel: 43 5583 2191
Fax: 43 5583 3330

BELGIUM (ANTWERP)
Firean Hotel
Karel Oomsstraat 6, 2018 Antwerp, Belgium
Tel: 32 3 237 02 60
Fax: 32 3 238 11 68

BELGIUM (BRUGES)
Hotel Acacia
Korte Zilverstraat 3A, 8000 Bruges, Belgium
Tel: 32 50 34 44 11
Fax: 32 50 33 88 17

BELGIUM (BRUGES)
Hotel Prinsenhof
Ontvangersstraat 9, 8000 Bruges, Belgium
Tel: 32 50 34 26 90
Fax: 32 50 34 23 21

BELGIUM (FLORENVILLE)
Hostellerie Le Prieuré De Conques
Rue de Conques 2, 6820 Florenville,
Belgium
Tel: 32 61 41 14 17
Fax: 32 61 41 27 03

BELGIUM (MALMEDY)
Hostellerie Trôs Marets
Route Des Trôs Marets, 4960 Malmédy,
Belgium
Tel: 32 80 33 79 17
Fax: 32 80 33 79 10

BELGIUM (MARCHE-EN-FAMENNE)
Château d'Hassonville
6900 Marche-en-Famenne, Belgium
Tel: 32 84 31 10 25
Fax: 32 84 31 60 27

BELGIUM (VIEUXVILLE)
Chateau de Palogne
Route du Palogne 3, 4190 Vieuxville,
Belgium
Tel: 32 86 21 38 74
Fax: 32 86 21 38 76

CYPRUS (LIMASSOL)
Le Meridien Limassol Spa and Resort
PO Box 56560, 3308 Limassol, Cyprus
Tel: 357 5 634 000
Fax: 357 5 634 222

CYPRUS (LIMASSOL)
Four Seasons Hotel
PO Box 57222, Limassol, Cyprus
Tel: 357 5 310 222
Fax: 357 5 310 887

CZECH REPUBLIC (PRAGUE)
Hotel Hoffmeister
Pod Bruskou 7, Kralov, 11800 Prague 1,
Czech Republic
Tel: 420 2 510 17 111
Fax: 420 2 510 17 100

CZECH REPUBLIC (PRAGUE)
Hotel U Krale Karla
Nerudova - Uvoz 4, 118 00 Prague 1, Czech
Republic
Tel: 420 2 575 31 211
Fax: 420 2 575 33 591

CZECH REPUBLIC (PRAGUE)
Sieber Hotel & Apartments
Slezska 55, 130 00 Prague 3, Czech Republic
Tel: 420 2 242 50 025
Fax: 420 2 242 50 027

DENMARK (FABORG)
Steensgaard Herregårdspension
Millinge, Steensgaard, 5600 Faaborg,
Denmark
Tel: 45 62 61 94 90
Fax: 45 63 61 78 61

DENMARK (NYBORG)

Hotel Hesselet

Christianslundsvej 119, 5800 Nyborg,
Denmark
Tel: 45 65 31 30 29
Fax: 45 65 31 29 58

ESTONIA (TALLINN)

Park Consul Schlössle

Pühavaimu 13-15, 10123 Tallinn, Estonia
Tel: 372 699 7700
Fax: 372 699 7777

FRANCE/ALPS (CHAMBÉRY-LE-VIEUX)

Château de Candie

Rue du Bois de Candie, 73000 Chambéry-le-
Vieux, France
Tel: 33 4 79 96 63 00
Fax: 33 4 79 96 63 10

FRANCE/ALPS (COURCHEVEL)

Hôtel Annapurna

73120 Courchevel 1850, France
Tel: 33 4 79 08 04 60
Fax: 33 4 79 08 15 31

FRANCE/ALPS (DIVONNE-LES-BAINS)

Le Domaine de Divonne

Avenue des Thermes, 01220 Divonne-les-
Bains, France
Tel: 33 4 50 40 34 34
Fax: 33 4 50 40 34 24

FRANCE/ALPS (LES GÊTS)

Chalet Hôtel La Marmotte

74 260 Les Gêts, France
Tel: 33 4 50 75 80 33
Fax: 33 4 50 75 83 26

FRANCE/ALPS (MEGÈVE)

Hôtel Mont-Blanc

Place de l'Eglise, 74120 Megève, France
Tel: 33 4 50 21 20 02
Fax: 33 4 50 21 45 28

FRANCE/ALPS (MEGÈVE)

Lodge Park Hôtel

100 Route d'Arly, 74120 Megève, France
Tel: 33 4 50 93 05 03
Fax: 33 4 50 93 09 52

FRANCE/ALPS (SCIEZ SUR LEMAN)

Château de Coudrée

Domaine de Coudrée, Bonnatrait, 74140
Sciez sur Leman, France
Tel: 33 4 50 72 62 33
Fax: 33 4 50 72 57 28

FRANCE/ALSACE-LORRAINE (COLMAR)

Hôtel Les Têtes

19 rue de Têtes, 68000 Colmar, France
Tel: 33 3 89 24 43 43
Fax: 33 3 89 24 58 34

FRANCE/ALSACE-LORRAINE (GÉRARDMER)

Hostellerie Les Bas Rupts

88400 Gérardmer, Vosges, France
Tel: 33 3 29 63 09 25
Fax: 33 3 29 63 00 40

FRANCE/BRITTANY (BILLIERS)

Domaine de Rochevilaine

Pointe de Pen Lan, 56190 Billiers, France
Tel: 33 2 97 41 61 61
Fax: 33 2 97 41 44 85

FRANCE/BRITTANY (LA GOUESNIERE/ST MALO)

Château de Bonaban

35350 La Gouesniere, France
Tel: 33 2 99 58 24 50
Fax: 33 2 99 58 28 41

FRANCE/BRITTANY (MOELAN-SUR-MER)

Manoir de Kertalg

Route de Riec sur Belon, 29350 Möelan-sur-
Mer, France
Tel: 33 2 98 39 77 77
Fax: 33 2 98 39 72 07

FRANCE/BRITTANY (PLEVEN)

Manoir du Vaumadeuc

22130 Pleven, France
Tel: 33 2 96 84 46 17
Fax: 33 2 96 84 40 16

FRANCE/BRITTANY (PLOERDUT)

Château du Launay

56160 Ploerdut, France
Tel: 33 2 97 39 46 32
Fax: 33 2 97 39 46 31

FRANCE/BURGUNDY (AVALLON)

Château de Vault de Lugny

11 Rue du Château, 89200 Avallon, France
Tel: 33 3 86 34 07 86
Fax: 33 3 86 34 16 36

FRANCE/BURGUNDY (AVALLON)

Hostellerie de la Poste

13 place Vauban, 89200 Avallon, France
Tel: 33 3 86 34 16 16
Fax: 33 3 86 34 19 19

FRANCE/BURGUNDY (BEAUNE)

Ermitage de Corton

R.N. 74, 21200 Chorey-les-Beaune, France
Tel: 33 3 80 22 05 28
Fax: 33 3 80 24 64 51

FRANCE/BURGUNDY (VILLEFARGEAU/AUXERRE)

Le Petit Manoir des Bruyères

Les Bruyères, 89240 Villefargeau, France
Tel: 33 3 86 41 32 82
Fax: 33 3 86 41 28 57

FRANCE/CHAMPAGNE (ÉPERNAY)

Hostellerie La Briqueterie

4 Route de Sézanne, 51530 Vinay-Epernay,
France
Tel: 33 3 26 59 99 99
Fax: 33 3 26 59 92 10

FRANCE/CHAMPAGNE (FÉRE-EN TARDENOIS)

Château de Fére

Route de Fismes, 02130 Fére-en-Tardenois,
France
Tel: 33 3 23 82 21 13
Fax: 33 3 23 82 37 81

FRANCE/CHAMPAGNE (TINQUEUX-REIMS)

L'Assiette Champenoise

40, Avenue Paul Vaillant Couturier, 51430
Tinqueux, France
Tel: 33 3 26 84 64 64
Fax: 33 3 26 04 15 69

FRANCE/LOIRE VALLEY (AMBOISE)

Château de Pray

Route de Chargé, 37400 Amboise, France
Tel: 33 2 47 57 23 67
Fax: 33 2 47 57 32 50

FRANCE/LOIRE VALLEY (AMBOISE)

Le Manoir des Minimes

34 Quai Charles Guinot, 37400 Amboise,
France
Tel: 33 2 47 30 40 40
Fax: 33 2 47 30 40 77

FRANCE/LOIRE VALLEY (LANGEAIS)

Château de Rochecotte

Saint Patrice, 37130 Langeais, France
Tel: 33 2 47 96 16 16
Fax: 33 2 47 96 90 59

FRANCE/LOIRE VALLEY (NOYANT DE TOURAINE)

Château de Brou

37800 Noyant de Touraine, France
Tel: 33 2 47 65 80 80
Fax: 33 2 47 65 82 92

FRANCE/LOIRE WEST (CHAMPIGNE)

Château des Briottières

49330 Champigné, France
Tel: 33 2 41 42 00 02
Fax: 33 2 41 42 01 55

FRANCE/LOIRE WEST (MISSILLAC)

Domaine de la Bretesche

44780 Missillac, France
Tel: 33 2 51 76 86 96
Fax: 33 2 40 66 99 47

FRANCE/NORMANDY (BREUIL-EN-BESSIN)

Château de Goville

14330 Le Breuil-en-Bessin, France
Tel: 33 2 31 22 19 28
Fax: 33 2 31 22 68 74

FRANCE/NORMANDY (ETRETAT)

Le Donjon

Chemin de Saint Claire, 76790 Etretat,
France
Tel: 33 2 35 27 08 23
Fax: 33 2 35 29 92 34

FRANCE/NORMANDY (FORGES-LES-EAUX)

Folie du Bois des Fontaines

Route de Dieppe, 76440 Forges-les-Eaux,
France
Tel: 33 2 32 89 50 68
Fax: 33 2 32 89 50 67

FRANCE/NORMANDY (HONFLEUR)

La Chaumière

Route du Littoral, 14600 Honfleur, France
Tel: 33 2 31 81 63 20
Fax: 33 2 31 89 59 23

FRANCE/NORMANDY (HONFLEUR)

La Ferme Saint-Siméon

Rue Adolphe-Marais, 14600 Honfleur,
France
Tel: 33 2 31 81 78 00
Fax: 33 2 2 31 89 48 48

FRANCE/NORMANDY (HONFLEUR)

Le Manoir du Butin

Phare du Butin, 14600 Honfleur, France
Tel: 33 2 31 81 63 00
Fax: 33 2 31 89 59 23

FRANCE/PARIS (CHAMPS-ELYSÉES)

Hôtel de la Trémoille

14 rue de la Trémoille, 75008 Paris, France
Tel: +33 1 47 23 34 20
Fax: +33 1 40 70 01 08

FRANCE/PARIS (CHAMPS-ELYSÉES)

Hôtel Franklin D. Roosevelt

18 rue Clement Marot, 75008 Paris, France
Tel: 33 1 53 57 49 50
Fax: 33 1 47 20 44 30

FRANCE/PARIS (CHAMPS-ELYSÉES)

Hôtel Plaza Athénée

25 Avenue Montaigne, 75008 Paris, France
Tel: 33 1 53 67 66 65
Fax: 33 1 53 67 66 66

FRANCE/PARIS(CHAMPS-ELYSEES)

Hôtel San Regis

12, rue Jean Goujon, 75008 Paris, France
Tel: 33 1 44 95 16 16
Fax: 33 1 45 61 05 48

FRANCE/PARIS (CONCORDE)

Hôtel de Crillon

10 Place de la Concorde, 75008 Paris,
France
Tel: 33 1 44 71 15 00
Fax: 33 1 44 71 15 02

FRANCE/PARIS (INVALIDES)

Hôtel Le Tourville

16 Avenue de Tourville, 75007 Paris, France
Tel: 33 1 47 05 62 62
Fax: 33 1 47 05 43 90

FRANCE/PARIS (MADELEINE)

Hôtel de L'Arcade

9 Rue de l'Arcade, 75008 Paris, France
Tel: 33 1 53 30 60 00
Fax: 33 1 40 07 03 07

FRANCE/PARIS (MADELEINE)

Hôtel le Lavoisier

21 rue Lavoisier, 75008 Paris, France
Tel: 33 1 53 30 06 06
Fax: 33 1 53 30 23 00

FRANCE/PARIS (PORTE MAILLOT)

L'Hôtel Pergolèse

3 Rue Pergolèse, 75116 Paris, France
Tel: 33 1 53 64 04 04
Fax: 33 1 53 64 04 40

FRANCE/PARIS (PORTE MAILLOT)

La Villa Maillot

143 Avenue de Malakoff, 75116 Paris,
France
Tel: 33 1 53 64 52 52
Fax: 33 1 45 00 60 61

FRANCE/PARIS (SAINT -GERMAN)

Hôtel le Saint-Grégoire

43 rue de l'Abbé Grégoire, 75006 Paris,
France
Tel: 33 1 45 48 23 23
Fax: 33 1 45 48 33 95

FRANCE/PARIS (SAINT-GERMAIN)

Hôtel Buci Latin

34 rue de Buci, 75006 Paris, France
Tel: 33 1 43 29 07 20
Fax: 33 1 43 29 67 44

FRANCE/PARIS-OUTSKIRTS (BOUTIGNY NR BARBIZON)

Domaine de Belesbat

Courdimanche-sur-Essonne, 91820
Boutigny-sur-Essonne, France
Tel: 33 1 69 23 19 00
Fax: 33 1 69 23 19 01

FRANCE/PARIS-OUTSKIRTS (GRESSY-EN-FRANCE/CHANTILLY)

Le Manoir de Gressy

77410 Gressy-en-France, France
Tel: 33 1 60 26 68 00
Fax: 33 1 60 26 45 46

FRANCE/POITOU-CHARENTES (CRAZANNES-SAINTES)

Château de Crazannes

17350 Crazannes, France
Tel: 33 6 80 65 40 96
Fax: 33 5 46 91 34 46

FRANCE/POITOU-CHARENTES (SAINT MAIXENT L'ECOLE)

Le Logis St Martin

Chemin de Pissot, 79400 St Maixent
L'Ecole, France
Tel: 33 5 49 05 58 68
Fax: 33 5 49 76 19 93

FRANCE/PROVENCE-CÔTE D'AZUR (BEAULIEU-SUR-MER)

La Réserve de Beaulieu

5 boulevard Général Leclerc, 06310
Beaulieu-sur-Mer, France
Tel: 33 4 93 01 00 01
Fax: 33 4 93 01 28 99

FRANCE/PROVENCE-CÔTE D'AZUR (EZE VILLAGE)

Château Eza

Rue de la Pise, 06360 Eze Village, France
Tel: 33 4 93 41 12 24
Fax: 33 4 93 41 16 64

FRANCE/PROVENCE-CÔTE D'AZUR (LES BAUX DE PROVENCE)

Mas de l'Oulivié

13 520 Les Baux de Provence, France
Tel: 33 4 90 54 35 78
Fax: 33 4 90 54 44 31

FRANCE/PROVENCE-COTE D'AZUR (LORGUES)

Château de Berne

Chemin de Berne, Flayosc, 83510 Lorgues,
France
Tel: 33 4 94 60 48 88
Fax: 33 4 94 60 48 89

FRANCE/PROVENCE-CÔTE D'AZUR (MANDELIEU-CANNES)

Ermitage du Riou

Avenue Henri Clews, 06210 Mandelieu-la-
Napoule, France
Tel: 33 4 93 49 95 56
Fax: 33 4 92 97 69 05

FRANCE/PROVENCE-CÔTE D'AZUR (MOUGINS-CANNES)

Le Mas Candille

Boulevard Rebuffel, 06250 Mougins, France
Tel: 33 4 92 28 43 43
Fax: 33 4 92 28 43 40

FRANCE/PROVENCE-CÔTE D'AZUR (RAMATUELLE)

La Ferme d'Augustin

Route de Tahiti, 83 350 Ramatuelle, France
Tel: 33 4 94 55 97 00
Fax: 33 4 94 97 40 30

FRANCE/PROVENCE-CÔTE D'AZUR (SAINT-PAUL-DE-VENCE)

Le Grande Bastide

Route de la Colle, 06570 Saint-Paul-de-
Vence, France
Tel: 33 4 93 32 50 30
Fax: 33 4 93 32 50 59

FRANCE/PROVENCE-CÔTE D'AZUR (SAINT-RÉMY-DE-PROVENCE)

Château des Alpilles

Route Départementale 31, Ancienne route
du Grés, 13210 St-Rémy-de-Provence
Tel: 33 4 90 92 03 33
Fax: 33 4 90 92 45 17

FRANCE/PROVENCE-CÔTE D'AZUR (SAINT-TROPEZ)

Hôtel Sube

15 Quai Suffren, 83990 Saint-Tropez, France
Tel: 33 4 94 97 30 04
Fax: 33 4 94 54 89 08

FRANCE/PROVENCE-CÔTE D'AZUR (SAINT TROPEZ)

La Résidence de la Pinède

Plage de la Bouillabaisse, 83990 Saint-Tropez, France
Tel: 33 4 94 55 91 00
Fax: 33 4 94 97 73 64

FRANCE/PROVENCE-CÔTE D'AZUR (SAINTE-MAXIME/BAY OF SAINT TROPEZ)

Hôtel Le Beauvallon

Baie de Saint-Tropez, Beauvallon-Grimaud, 83120 Sainte-Maxime, France
Tel: 33 4 94 55 78 88
Fax: 33 4 94 55 78 78

FRANCE/PROVENCE-CÔTE D'AZUR (SERRE-CHEVALIER)

L'Auberge du Choucas

Serre-Chevalier 1500, 05220 Monetier-les-Bains, France
Tel: 33 4 92 24 42 73
Fax: 33 4 92 24 51 60

FRANCE/PROVENCE-CÔTE D'AZUR (UZÉS)

Château d'Arpaillagues

Hôtel Marie d'Agoult, 30 700 Uzés, France
Tel: 33 4 66 22 14 48
Fax: 33 4 66 22 56 10

FRANCE/CORSICA (PORTICCIO)

Hôtel Le Maquis

BP 94, 20166 Porticcio-Corsica, France
Tel: 33 4 95 25 05 55
Fax: 33 4 95 25 11 70

FRANCE/RHÔNE VALLEY (GRIGNAN)

Manoir de la Roseraie

Route de Valréas, 26230 Grignan, France
Tel: 33 4 75 46 58 15
Fax: 33 4 75 46 91 55

FRANCE/RHÔNE VALLEY (LYON)

La Tour Rose

22 rue du Boeuf, 69005 Lyon, France
Tel: 33 4 78 37 25 90
Fax: 33 4 78 42 26 02

FRANCE/SOUTH WEST (BIARRITZ)

Hôtel du Palais

Avenue de l'Impératrice, 64200 Biarrritz, France
Tel: 33 5 59 41 64 00
Fax: 33 5 59 41 67 99

FRANCE/SOUTH WEST (CASTRES)

Château d'Aiguefonde

Rue du Château, 81200 Aiguefonde, France
Tel: 33 5 63 98 13 70
Fax: 33 5 63 98 69 90

GERMANY (BADENWEILER)

Hotel Römerbad

Schlossplatz 1, 79410 Badenweiler, Germany
Tel: 49 7632 700
Fax: 49 7632 70200

GERMANY (MUNICH)

Hotel Königshof

Karlsplatz 25, 80335 Munich, Germany
Tel: 49 8955 1360
Fax: 49 8955 136113

GERMANY (OBERWESEL/RHEIN)

Burghotel Auf Schönburg

55430 Oberwesel/Rhein, Germany
Tel: 49 6744 93930
Fax: 49 6744 1613

GERMANY (ROTHENBURG OB DER TAUBER)

Hotel Eisenhut

Herrngasse 3-7, 91541 Rothenburg ob der Tauber, Germany
Tel: 49 9861 7050
Fax: 49 9861 70545

GERMANY (SYLT)

Christian VIII

Heleeker 1, 25980 Archsum/Sylt, Germany
Tel: 49 4651 97070
Fax: 49 4651 970777

GERMANY (SYLT)

Landhaus Nösse

Nösistieg 13, Morsum 25980 Sylt, Germany
Tel: 49 4651 9722 0
Fax: 49 4651 891658

GERMANY (SYLT)

Hotel Restaurant Jörg Müller

Süderstrasse 8, 25980 Westerland/Sylt, Germany
Tel: 49 4651 27788
fax: 49 4651 201 471

GERMANY (TRIBERG)

Romantik Parkhotel Wehrle

Gartenstr.24, 78094 Triberg, Germany
Tel: 49 7722 86020
Fax: 49 7722 860290

GERMANY (WASSENBERG)

Hotel Burg Wassenberg

Kirchstrasse 17, 41849 Wassenberg, Germany
Tel: 49 2432 9490
Fax: 49 2432 949100

GIBRALTAR

The Rock Hotel

3 Europa Road, Gibraltar
Tel: 350 73 000
Fax: 350 73 513

The Atlantic Hotel

La Moye, St Brelade, Jersey JE3 8HE,
Channel Islands
Tel: 44 1534 44101
Fax: 44 1534 44102

Adare Manor Hotel & Golf Resort

Adare, Co Limerick, Ireland
Tel: 353 61 396 566
Fax: 353 61 396 124

Waren House

Waren Mill, Bamburgh, Northumberland
NE70 7EE, England
Tel: 44 1668 214581
Fax: 44 1668 214484

Risley Hall

Derby Rd, Risley, Derbyshire DE72 3SS,
England
Tel: 44 115 939 9000
Fax: 44 115 939 7766

Hoar Cross Hall Health Spa Resort

Hoar Cross, Nr Yoxall, Staffordshire DE13
8QS, England
Tel: 44 1283 575671
Fax: 44 1283 575652

The Academy, The Bloomsbury Townhouse

21 Gower Street, London WC1E 6HG,
England
Tel: 44 20 7631 4115
Fax: 44 20 7636 3442

The Beaufort

33 Beaufort Gardens, Knightsbridge, London
SW3 1PP, England
Tel: 44 20 7584 5252
Fax: 44 20 7589 2834

Beaufort House Apartments

45 Beaufort Gardens, London SW3 1PN,
England
Tel: 44 20 7584 2600
Fax: 44 20 7584 6532

Brown's Hotel

Albermarle Street, London W1X 4BP,
England
Tel: 44 20 7493 6020
Fax: 44 20 7493 9381

Cannizaro House

West Side, Wimbledon Common, London
SW19 4UE, England
Tel: 44 20 8879 1464
Fax: 44 20 8879 7338

The Colonnade, The Little Venice Town House

2 Warrington Crescent, London W9 1ER,
England
Tel: 44 20 7286 1052
Fax: 44 20 7286 1057

The Dorchester

Park Lane, Mayfair, London WIA 2HJ,
England
Tel: 44 20 7629 8888
Fax: 44 20 7409 0114

Draycott House Apartments

10 Draycott Avenue, Chelsea, London SW3
3AA, England
Tel: 44 20 7584 4659
Fax: 44 20 7225 3694

The Halcyon

81 Holland Park, London W11 3RZ,
England
Tel: 44 20 7727 7288
Fax: 44 20 7229 5816

The Leonard

15 Seymour Street, London W1H 5AA,
England
Tel: 44 20 7935 2010
Fax: 44 20 7935 6700

The Milestone

1-2 Kensington Court, London W8 5DL,
England
Tel: 44 20 7917 1000
Fax: 44 20 7917 1010

Number Eleven Cadogan Gardens

11 Cadogan Gardens, Sloane Square,
London SW3 2RJ, England
Tel: 44 20 7730 7000
Fax: 44 20 7730 5217

Number Sixteen

16 Sumner Place, London SW7 3EG,
England
Tel: 44 20 7589 5232
Fax: 44 20 7584 8615

Pembridge Court Hotel

34 Pembridge Gardens, London W2 4DX,
England
Tel: 44 20 7229 9977
Fax: 44 20 7727 4982

Shaw Park Plaza

100-110 Euston Road, London NW1 2AJ,
England
Tel: 44 20 7666 9000
Fax: 44 20 7666 9100

GREAT BRITAIN & IRELAND (LONDON)

Sloane Hotel

29 Draycott Place, Chelsea, London SW3
2SH, England
Tel: 44 20 7581 5757
Fax: 44 20 7584 1348

GREAT BRITAIN & IRELAND (LONDON)

The Lexham Apartments

32-38 Lexham Gardens, Kensington,
London W8 5JE, England
Tel: 44 20 7559 4444
Fax: 44 20 7559 4400

GREAT BRITAIN & IRELAND (LONDON)

The Rookery

Peter's Lane, Cowcross Street, London
EC1M 6DS, England
Tel: 44 20 7336 0931
Fax: 44 20 7336 0932

GREAT BRITAIN & IRELAND (WINDERMERE)

Miller Howe

Rayrigg Road, Windermere, Cumbria LA23
1EY, England
Tel: 44 15394 42536
Fax: 44 15394 45664

GREECE (ATHENS)

Hotel Pentelikon

66 Diligianni Street, 14562 Athens, Greece
Tel: 30 162 30650 6
Fax: 30 1 80 10 314

GREECE (CRETE)

St Nicolas Bay Hotel

Agios Nikolaos, 72100 Crete, Greece
Tel: 30 841 25041
Fax: 30 841 24556

GREECE (KARPENISI)

Hotel Club Montana

36100 Karpenissi, Greece
Tel: 30 237 80400
Fax: 30 237 80409

GREECE (SAMOS ISLAND)

Doryssa Bay Hotel-Village

83103 Pythagorion, Samos Island, Aegean
Island, Greece
Tel: 30 273 61 360
Fax: 30 273 614 63

HUNGARY (BUDAPEST)

Danubius Hotel Gellért

St.Gellért Tér 1, 1111 Budapest, Hungary
Tel: 36 1 385 2200
Fax: 36 1 466 6631

ITALY/CAMPANIA (POSITANO)

Romantik Hotel Poseidon

Via Pasitea 148, 84017 Positano, Italy
Tel: 39 089 81 11 11
Fax: 39 089 87 58 33

ITALY/CAMPANIA (SORRENTO)

Grand Hotel Cocumella

Via Cocumella 7, 80065 Sant'Agnello,
Sorrento, Italy
Tel: 39 081 87 82 933
Fax: 39 081 87 83 712

ITALY/CAMPANIA (SORRENTO)

Grand Hotel Excelsior Vittoria

Piazza Tasso 34, Sorrento-(Naples), Italy
Tel: 39 081 80 71 044
Fax: 39 081 87 71 206

ITALY/EMILIA ROMAGNA (BAGNO DI ROMAGNA)

Hotel Tosco Romagnolo

Piazza Dante Alighieri 2, 47021 Bagno di
Romagna, Italy
Tel: 39 054 39 11 260
Fax: 39 054 39 11 014

ITALY/EMILIA ROMAGNA (CASTELLO DI MONTEGRIDOLFO)

Palazzo Vivani Castello Di Montegridolfo

Via Roma 38, 47837 Montegridolfo, Italy
Tel: 39 0541 85 53 50
Fax: 39 0541 85 53 40

ITALY/EMILIA ROMAGNA (FERRARA)

Albergo Annunziata

Piazza Repubblica 5, 44100 Ferrara, Italy
Tel: 39 0532 20 11 11
Fax: 39 0532 20 32 33

ITALY/EMILIA ROMAGNA (FERRARA)

Ripagrande Hotel

Via Ripagrande 21, 44100 Ferrara, Italy
Tel: 39 053 27 65 250
Fax: 39 053 27 64 377

ITALY/LAZIO (PALO LAZIALE-ROME)

La Posta Vecchia

Palo Laziale, 00055 Ladispoli (Rome), Italy
Tel: 39 069 94 95 01
Fax: 39 069 94 95 07

ITALY/LAZIO (ROME)

Hotel Farnese

Via Alessandro Farnese 30, (Angolo Viale
Giulio Cesare), 00192 Rome, Italy
Tel: 39 063 21 25 53
Fax: 39 063 21 51 29

ITALY/LAZIO (ROME)

Hotel Giulio Cesare

Via Degli Scipioni 287, 00192 Rome, Italy
Tel: 39 063 21 07 51
Fax: 39 063 21 17 36

ITALY/LAZIO (ROME)

Romantik Hotel Barocco

Piazza Barberini 9, 00187 Rome, Italy
Tel: 39 064 87 20 01
Fax: 39 064 85 994

ITALY/LIGURIA (FINALE LIGURE)

Hotel Punta Est

Via Aurelia 1, 17024 Finale Ligure, Italy
Tel: 39 019 60 06 11
Fax: 39 019 60 06 11

ITALY/LIGURIA (SESTRI LEVANTE)

Grand Hotel Villa Balbi

Viale Rimembranza 1, 16039 Sestri Levante, Italy
Tel: 39 018 54 29 41
Fax: 39 018 54 82 459

ITALY/LOMBARDY (COMO)

Albergo Terminus

Lungo Lario Trieste 14, 22100 Como, Italy
Tel: 39 031 32 91 11
Fax: 39 031 30 25 50

ITALY/LOMBARDY (COMO)

Hotel Villa Flori

Via Cernobbio 12, 22100 Como, Italy
Tel: 39 031 57 31 05
Fax: 39 031 57 03 79

ITALY/LOMBARDY (MANTOVA)

Albergo San Lorenzo

Piazza Concordia 14, 46100 Mantova, Italy
Tel: 39 037 62 20 500
Fax: 39 037 63 27 194

ITALY/LOMBARDY (MILAN)

Capitol Millennium

Via Cimarosa 6, 20144 Milan, Italy
Tel: 39 024 38 591
Fax: 39 024 69 47 24

ITALY/LOMBARDY (MILAN)

Hotel Auriga

Via Pirelli 7, 20124 Milan, Italy
Tel: 39 026 69 85 851
Fax: 39 026 69 80 698

ITALY/PIEDMONT (NOVI LIGURE)

Relais Villa Pomela

Via Serravalle 69, 15067 Novi Ligure, Italy
Tel: 39 014 33 29 910
Fax: 39 014 33 29 912

ITALY/PIEDMONT (TORINO)

Hotel Victoria

Via N.Costa 4, 10123 Torino, Italy
Tel: 39 011 56 11 909
Fax: 39 011 56 11 806

ITALY/SCICLY (ETNA)

Hotel Villa Paradiso Dell' Etna

Via per Viagrande 37, 95037 SG La Punta, Italy
Tel: 39 095 75 12 409
Fax: 39 095 74 13 861

ITALY/SICILY (GIARDINI NAXOS)

Hellenia Yachting Hotel

Via Jannuzzo 41, 98035 Giardini Naxos, Italy
Tel: 39 094 25 17 37
Fax: 39 094 25 43 10

ITALY/SICILY (MARINA D'AGRO)

Hotel Baia Taormina

Statale dello Jonio 39, 98030 Marina d'Agro, Italy
Tel: 39 094 27 56 292
Fax: 39 094 27 56 603

ITALY/SICILY (SIRACUSA)

Hotel Roma

Via Minerva 10, 96100 Siracusa, Italy
Tel: 39 093 14 65 626
Fax: 39 093 14 65 535

ITALY/SICILY (TAORMINA MARE)

Hotel Villa Sant' Andrea

Via Nazionale 137, 98030 Taormina Mare, Italy
Tel: 39 094 22 31 25
Fax: 39 094 22 48 38

ITALY/SOUTH TYROL (MARLING-MÉRAN)

Romantik Hotel Oberwirt

St Felixweg 2, 39020 Marling/Méran, Italy
Tel: 39 047 34 47 111
Fax: 39 047 34 47 130

ITALY/SOUTH TYROL (MAULS)

Romantik Hotel Stafler

Mauls 10, 39040 Freienfeld, Italy
Tel: 39 047 27 71 136
Fax: 39 047 27 71 094

ITALY/SOUTH TYROL(MERANO)

Park Hotel Mignon

Via Grabmayr 5, 39012 Merano, Italy
Tel: 39 047 32 30 353
Fax: 39 047 32 30 644

ITALY/SOUTH TYROL (NOVA LEVANTE)

Posthotel Weisses Rössl

Via Carezza 30, 39056 Nova Levante, Dolomites, Italy
Tel: 39 047 16 13 113
Fax: 39 047 16 13 390

ITALY/SOUTH TYROL (SAN CANDINO)

Parkhotel Sole Paradiso

Via Haunold 8, 39038 San Candino, Italy
Tel: 39 047 49 13 120
Fax: 39 047 49 13 193

ITALY/SOUTH TYROL (VÖLS AM SCHLERN)

Romantik Hotel Turm

Piazza della Chiesa 9, 39050 Fie ollo Sciliar, Italy
Tel: 39 047 17 25 014
Fax: 39 047 17 25 474

ITALY/TUSCANY (CASTELLINA IN CHIANTI)

Romantik Hotel Tenuta Di Ricavo

Localita Ricavo 4, 53011 Castellina In Chianti, Italy
Tel: 39 057 77 40 221
Fax: 39 057 77 41 014

ITALY/TRENTINO (MADONNA DI CAMPIGLIO)

Hotel Lorenzetti

Via Dolomiti di Brenta 119, 38084 Madonna Di Campiglio, Italy
Tel: 39 046 54 41 404
Fax: 39 046 54 40 688

ITALY/TUSCANY (CINQUALE-FORTE DEI MARMI)

Hotel Villa Undulna

Viale Marina, 54030 Cinquale Di Montignoso, Italy
Tel: 39 058 58 07 788
Fax: 39 058 58 07 791

ITALY/TUSCANY (FLORENCE)

Hotel J and J

Via Mezzo 20, 50121 Florence, Italy
Tel: 39 055 26 31 21
Fax: 39 055 24 02 82

ITALY/TUSCANY (FLORENCE)

Hotel Montebello Splendid

Via Montebello 60, 50123 Florence, Italy
Tel: 39 055 23 98 051
Fax: 39 055 21 18 67

ITALY/TUSCANY (GAIOLE IN CHIANTI)

Castello Di Spaltenna

Loc. Pieve di Spaltenna, 53013 Gaiole in Chianti, Italy
Tel: 39 057 77 49 483
Fax: 39 057 77 49 269

ITALY/TUSCANY (PIEVESCOLA)

Hotel Relais La Suvera

53030 Pievescola, Siena, Italy
Tel: 39 057 79 60 300
Fax: 39 057 79 60 220

ITALY/TUSCANY (PORTO ERCOLE)

Il Pellicano

Localita lo Sbarcatello, 58018 Porto Ercole, Italy
Tel: 39 056 48 58 111
Fax: 39 056 48 33 418

ITALY/UMBRIA (ASSISI)

Romantik Hotel Le Silve di Armenzano

Loc. Armenzano, 06081 Assisi, Italy
Tel: 39 075 80 19 000
Fax: 39 075 80 19 005

ITALY/VENETIA (VENICE LIDO)

Albergo Quattro Fontane

Via Quattro Fontane 16, 30126 Lido di Venezia, Italy
Tel: 39 041 52 60 227
Fax: 39 041 52 60 726

LATVIA (RIGA)

Hotel de Rome

Kalkuiela 28, 1050 Riga, Latvia
Tel: 371 708 7600
Fax: 371 708 76 06

LATVIA (RIGA)

Hotel Grand Palace

Pils Iela 12, 1050 Riga, Latvia
Tel: 371 704 4000
Fax: 371 704 4001

LATVIA (RIGA)

Hotel Konventa Seta

Kaleju str 9/11, 1050 Riga, Latvia
Tel: 371 708 7501
Fax: 371 708 7515

LUXEMBOURG (REMICH)

Hotel Saint Nicolas

31 Esplanade, 5533 Remich, Luxembourg
Tel: 352 26 663
Fax: 352 26 66 36 66

MONACO (MONTE CARLO)

Monte-Carlo Beach Hotel

Avenue Princesse Grace, 06190 Roquebrune-Cap-Martin, France
Tel: 33 4 93 28 66 66
Fax: 33 4 93 78 14 18

MONACO (MONTE-CARLO)

Hôtel Hermitage

Square Beaumarchais, MC 98005, Monaco
Tel: 377 92 16 40 00
Fax: 377 92 16 38 52

NETHERLANDS (AMSTERDAM)

Ambassade Hotel

Herengracht 341, 1016 AZ Amsterdam, Netherlands
Tel: 31 205 55 02 22
Fax: 31 205 55 02 77

NETHERLANDS (AMSTERDAM)

The Canal House Hotel

Keizersgracht 148, 1015 CX, Amsterdam, The Netherlands
Tel: 31 206 22 51 82
Fax: 31 206 24 13 17

NETHERLANDS (AMSTERDAM)

Seven One Seven

Prinsengracht 717, 1017 JW, Amsterdam, The Netherlands
Tel: 31 204 27 07 17
Fax: 31 204 23 07 17

NETHERLANDS (DE LUTTE)

Landhuishotel & Restaurant Bloemenbeek

Beuninger Straat 6, 7587 ZG De Lutte, The Netherlands
Tel: 31 541 55 12 24
Fax: 31 541 55 22 85

NETHERLANDS (DRUNEN)

Hotel De Duinrand

Steergerf 2, 5151 RB Drunen, The
Netherlands
Tel: 31 416 37 24 98
Fax: 31 416 37 49 19

NETHERLANDS (MOLENHOEK)

Jachtslot de Mookerheide

Heumensebaan 2, 6584 CL Molenhoek, The
Netherlands
Tel: 31 243 58 30 35
Fax: 31 243 58 43 55

NETHERLANDS (OOTMARSUM)

Hotel de Wiemsel

Winhofflaan 2, 7631 HX Ootmarsum, The
Netherlands
Tel: 31 541 29 21 55
Fax: 31 541 29 32 95

NETHERLANDS (VOORBURG)

Restaurant Hotel Savelberg

Oosteinde 14, 2271 EH Voorburg, The
Netherlands
Tel: 31 703 872 081
Fax: 31 703 87 77 15

NORWAY (DALEN)

Dalen Hotel

PO Boks 123, 3880 Dalen, Norway
Tel: 47 35 07 70 00
Fax: 47 35 07 70 11

NORWAY (MOSS)

Hotel Refsnes Gods

P.O Box 236, 1501 Moss, Norway
Tel: 47 69 27 83 00
Fax: 47 69 27 83 01

NORWAY (OSLO)

First Hotel Bastion

Skippergaten 7, 0152 Oslo, Norway
Tel: 47 22 47 77 00
Fax: 47 22 33 11 80

NORWAY (SANDANE)

Gloppen Hotel

6860 Sandane, Norway
Tel: 47 57 86 53 33
Fax: 47 57 86 60 02

NORWAY (SOLVORN)

Walaker Hotell

6879 Solvorn, Norway
Tel: 47 57 68 42 07
Fax: 47 57 68 45 44

NORWAY (VOSS)

Fleischers Hotel

5700 Voss, Norway
Tel: 47 56 52 05 00
Fax: 47 56 32 05 01

PORTUGAL (ALIJÓ)

Pousada De Alijó- Barâo de Forrester

5070 031 Alijó, Portugal
Tel: 351 259 95 92 15
Fax: 351 259 95 93 04

PORTUGAL (CARVOEIRO)

Casa Domilu

Estrada de Benagil, Apartado 1250, Praia do
Carvoeiro, 8400 Lagoa, Portugal
Tel: 351 282 358 404
Fax: 351 823 282 358 410

PORTUGAL (CHAVES)

Forte de S. Francisco Hotel

Alto da Pedisquera, 5400 Chaves, Portugal
Tel: 351 276 33 37 00
Fax: 351 276 33 37 01

PORTUGAL (CONDEIXA-A-NOVA)

Pousada de Condeixa-a-Nova Santa Cristina

3150-142 Condeixa-a-Nova, Portugal
Tel: 351 239 94 12 86
Fax: 351 239 94 30 97

PORTUGAL (ESTOI)

Monte do Casal

Cerro do Lobo Estoi, 8000 Faro, Algarve,
Portugal
Tel: 351 289 99 01 40
Fax: 351 289 99 13 41

PORTUGAL (LAGOS)

Romantik Hotel Vivenda Miranda

Porto de Mós, 8600 Lagos, Algarve, Portugal
Tel: 351 282 763 222
Fax: 351 282 760 342

PORTUGAL (MADEIRA)

Quinta Da Bela Vista

Caminho do Avista Navios 4, 9000 Funchal,
Madeira, Portugal
Tel: 351 291 70 64 00
Fax: 351 291 70 64 11

PORTUGAL (MADEIRA)

Reid's Palace

9000-098 Funchal, Madeira, Portugal
Tel: 351 291 71 71 71
Fax: 351 291 71 71 77

PORTUGAL (MANGUALDE)

Casa D'Azurara

Rua Nova, nr 78, 3530 Mangualde, Portugal
Tel: 351 232 61 20 10
Fax: 351 232 62 25 75

PORTUGAL (REDONDO)

Convento de Sao Paulo

Aldeia da Serra, 7170 Redondo, Portugal
Tel: 351 266 98 91 60
Fax: 351 266 99 91 04

PORTUGAL (SÃO BRÁS DE ALPORTEL)

Pousada de São Brás de Alportel

8150-054 São Brás de Alportel, Portugal
Tel: 351 28 98 42 305
Fax: 351 289 84 17 26

PORTUGAL (VILA VIÇOSA- D.JOÃO IV

Pousada De Vila Viçosa-D.João IV

7160 Vila Viçosa, Portugal
Tel: 351 268 98 07 42
Fax: 351 268 98 07 47

SPAIN/ANDALUCIA (ALMUÑECAR)

Hotel Suites Albayzin Del Mar

Avenida Costa del Sol 23, 18690
Almuñecar, (Granada), Spain
Tel: 34 958 63 21 61
Fax: 34 958 63 12 37

SPAIN/ANDALUCIA (ARCOS DE LA FRONTERA)

Hacienda El Santiscal

Avda. del Santiscal 129 (Lago de Arcos),
11630 Arcos de la Frontera, Spain
Tel: 34 956 70 83 13
Fax: 34 956 70 82 68

SPAIN/ANDALUCIA (MALAGA)

La Posada Del Torcal

29230 Villanueva de la Concepción, Malaga,
Spain
Tel: 34 952 03 11 77
Fax: 34 952 03 10 06

SPAIN/ANDALUCIA (MARBELLA)

Hotel Puente Romano

P.O Box 204, 29600 Marbella, Spain
Tel: 34 952 82 09 00
Fax: 34 952 82 26 43

SPAIN/ANDALUCIA (MARBELLA)

Marbella Club Hotel,Golf and Spa Resort

Boulevard Príncipe Alfonso von Hohenlohe
s/n, 29600 Marbella, Spain
Tel: 34 952 82 22 11
Fax: 34 952 82 98 84

SPAIN/ANDALUCIA (MARBELLA/ESTEPONA)

Las Dunas Suites

Ctra de Cádiz, Km163.5, 29689 Marbella-
Estepona, Malaga, Spain
Tel: 34 952 79 43 45
Fax: 34 952 79 48 25

SPAIN/ANDALUCIA (MIJAS-COSTA)

Hotel Byblos Andaluz

Mijas Golf, Apt.138, 29640 Fuengirola
(Malaga), Spain
Tel: 34 95 246 0250
Fax: 34 952 256 9582

SPAIN/ANDALUCIA (PUERTO DE SANTA MARIA-CÁDIZ)

Monasterio de San Miguel

Calte Larga 27, 11500 El Puerto de Santa
Maria, Cádiz, Spain
Tel: 34 956 54 04 40
Fax: 34 956 54 26 04

SPAIN/ANDALUCIA (SEVILLE)

Cortijo Aguila Real

Crta.Guillena-Burguillos, KM4, 41210
Guillena, Seville, Spain
Tel: 34 955 78 50 06
Fax: 34 955 78 43 30

SPAIN/ANDALUCIA (SEVILLE)

Hacienda Benazuza

41800 Sanlúcar la Mayor, Seville, Spain
Tel: 34 955 70 33 44
Fax: 34 955 70 34 10

SPAIN/ANDALUCIA (SOTOGRANDE)

Almenara Hotel - Golf

Avenida Almenara s/n
11310, Sotogrande, Spain
Tel: 34 956 58 20 00
Fax: 34 956 58 20 01

SPAIN/ARAGON (TERUEL)

La Parada Del Compte

Antigua Estación de Ferrocarril, 44597 Torre
del Compte, Teruel, Spain
Tel: 34 978 76 90 72
Fax: 34 978 76 90 74

SPAIN/BALEARIC ISLANDS (MALLORCA)

Ca's Xorc

Carretera de Deia, km 56.1, 07100 Soller,
Mallorca, Spain
Tel: 34 971 63 80 91
Fax: 34 971 63 38 20

SPAIN/BALEARIC ISLANDS (MALLORCA)

Hotel Monnaber Nou

Possessio Monnaber Nou, 07310 Campanet,
Mallorca, Spain
Tel: 34 971 87 71 76
Fax: 34 971 87 71 27

SPAIN/BALEARIC ISLANDS (MALLORCA)

Hotel Vistamar De Valldemosa

Ctra. Valldemosa, Andratx Km 2, 07170
Valldemosa, Mallorca, Spain
Tel: 34 971 61 23 00
Fax: 34 971 61 25 83

SPAIN/BALEARIC ISLANDS (MALLORCA)

Hotel Sa Pedrissa

Crta Valldemosa Deia Km 64, 5, 07179
Mallorca, Spain
Tel: 34 971 63 91 11
Fax: 34 971 63 94 56

SPAIN/CANARY ISLANDS (TENERIFE)

Gran Hotel Bahia Del Duque

38660 Adeje, Costa Adeje, Tenerife South,
Spain
Tel: 34 922 74 69 00
Fax: 34 922 74 69 25

SPAIN/CANARY ISLANDS (TENERIFE)

Hotel Botánico

Avda. Richard J. Yeoward 1, 38400 Puerto
de la Cruz, Tenerife, Spain
Tel: 34 922 38 14 00
Fax: 34 922 38 15 04

SPAIN/CANARY ISLANDS (TENERIFE)

Hotel Jardin Tropical

Calle Gran Bretana, 38670 Costa Adeje,
Tenerife, Spain
Tel: 34 922 74 60 00
Fax: 34 922 74 60 60

SPAIN/CANARY ISLANDS (TENERIFE)

Hotel San Roque

C/. Esteban de Ponte 32, 38450 Garachico,
Tenerife, Spain
Tel: 34 922 13 34 35
Fax: 34 922 13 34 06

SPAIN/CASTILLE (SALAMANCA)

Hotel Rector

Rector Esperabe, 10-Apartado 399, 37008
Salamanca, Spain
Tel: 34 923 21 84 82
Fax: 34 923 21 40 08

SPAIN/CATALONIA (BARCELONA)

Hotel Claris

Pau Claris 150, 08009 Barcelona, Spain
Tel: 34 934 87 62 62
Fax: 34 932 15 79 70

SPAIN/CATALONIA (BARCELONA)

Hotel Colon

Avenida de la Catedral 7, 08002 Barcelona,
Spain
Tel: 34 933 01 14 04
Fax: 34 933 17 29 15

SPAIN/CATALONIA (BARCELONA)

The Gallery

Rosselló 249, 08008 Barcelona, Spain
Tel: 34 93 415 99 11
Fax: 34 93 415 91 84

SPAIN/CATALONIA (CAMPRODON)

Hotel Grevol

Crta. Camprodon a Setcases s/n, 17869
Llanars, Spain
Tel: 34 972 74 10 13
Fax: 34 972 74 10 87

SPAIN/CATALONIA (LLORET DE MAR)

Hotel Rigat Park

Playa de Fenals, 17310 Lloret de Mar, Costa
Brava, Spain
Tel: 34 972 36 52 00
Fax: 34 972 37 04 11

SPAIN/CATALONIA (PALS)

Hotel La Costa

Avenida Arenales de Mar 3, 17526 Platja de
Pals, Costa Brava, Spain
Tel: 34 972 66 77 40
Fax: 34 972 66 77 36

SPAIN/CATALONIA (SITGES)

Hotel Estela Barcelona

Avda. Port d'Aiguadolc s/n, 08870 Stiges
(Barcelona), Spain
Tel: 34 938 11 45 45
Fax: 34 938 11 45 46

SPAIN/CATALONIA (TARRAGONA)

Hotel Termes Montbrío Resort, Spa & Park

Carrer Nou 38, 43340 Montbrío del Camp,
Tarragona, Spain
Tel: 34 977 81 40 00
Fax: 34 977 82 62 51

SPAIN/CATALONIA (VILADRAU)

Xalet La Coromina

Carretera De Vic s/n, 17406, Viladrau, Spain
Tel: 34 938 84 92 64
Fax: 34 938 84 81 60

SPAIN/MADRID (MADRID)

Villa Real

Plaza de las Cortes 10, 28014 Madrid, Spain
Tel: 34 914 20 37 67
Fax: 34 914 20 25 47

SWEDEN (BORGHOLM)

Halltorps Gästgiveri

387 92 Borgholm, Gastgiveri, Sweden
Tel: 46 485 85 000
Fax: 46 485 85 001

SWEDEN (GOTHENBURG)

Hotel Eggers

Drottningtorget, Box 323, 401 25
Gothenburg, Sweden
Tel: 46 318 06 070
Fax: 46 311 54 243

SWEDEN (LAGAN)

Toftaholm Herrgård

Toftaholm P.A., 34014 Lagan, Sweden
Tel: 46 370 44 055
Fax: 46 370 44 045

SWEDEN (SÖDERKÖPING)

Romantik Hotel Söderköpings Brunn

Skönbergagatan 35, Box 44, 614 21
Söderköping, Sweden
Tel: 46 121 10 900
Fax: 46 121 13 941

SWEDEN (TÄLLBERG)

Romantik Hotel Åkerblads

793 70 Tällberg, Sweden
Tel: 46 247 50 800
Fax: 46 247 50 652

SWITZERLAND (BURGDORF-BERN)

Hotel Stadthaus

Kirchbühl 2, 3402 Burgdorf-Bern,
Switzerland
Tel: 41 34 428 8000
Fax: 41 34 428 8008

SWITZERLAND (CHATEAU D'OEX)

Hostellerie Bon Accueil

1837 Chateau d'Oex, Switzerland
Tel: 41 26 924 6320
Fax: 41 26 924 5126

SWITZERLAND (GSTAAD)

Le Grand Chalet

Neueretstrasse, 3780 Gstaad, Switzerland
Tel: 41 33 748 7676
Fax: 41 33 748 7677

SWITZERLAND (KANDERSTEG)

Royal Park ***** Hotel

3718 Kandersteg, Switzerland
Tel: 41 33 675 8888
Fax: 41 33 675 8880

SWITZERLAND (ZERMATT)

Grand Hotel Zermatterhof

3920 Zermatt, Switzerland
Tel: 41 27 966 6600
Fax: 41 27 966 6699

SWITZERLAND (ZUOZ)

Posthotel Engiadina

Via Maistra, 7524 Zuoz, Switzerland
Tel: 41 81 854 1021
Fax: 41 81 854 3303

TURKEY (ANTALYA)

Marina Residence and Restaurant

Mermerli Sokak, No 15 Kalegi, 07100
Antalya, Turkey
Tel: 90 242 247 5490
Fax: 90 242 241 1765

TURKEY (FETHIYE-MUGLA)

Hillside Beach Club

Kalemya Koyu, Po Box 123, Fethiye/ Mugla,
Turkey
Tel: 90 252 614 8360
Fax: 90 252 614 1470

TURKEY (KALKAN)

Hotel Villa Mahal

P.K 4 Kalkan, 07960 Antalya, Turkey
Tel: 90 242 844 3268
Fax: 90 242 844 2122

TURKEY (KAS)

Savile Residence

Cukurbag Yarimidasi, Kas,Antalya, Turkey
Tel: 90 242 836 2300
UK Tel: 44 207 625 3001

MINI LISTINGS

Johansens Recommended Hotels & Inns – North America, Bermuda, The Caribbean 2001

Here in brief are the entries that appear in full in Johansens Recommended Hotels & Inns – North America, Bermuda, The Caribbean 2001.
To order Johansens guides turn to the order forms at the back of this book.

BERMUDA (HAMILTON)

Rosedon Hotel

PO Box HM 290, Hamilton HMAX,
Bermuda
Tel: 1 441 295 1640
Fax: 1 441 295 5904

CARIBBEAN (MARTINIQUE)

Fregate Bleu

Quartier Fregate Vauclin Rd, 97240 Le
Francois, Martinique
Tel: 596 54 54 66
Fax: 596 54 78 48

BERMUDA (PAGET)

Fourways Inn

PO Box PG 294, Paget PG BX, Bermuda
Tel: 1 441 236 6517
Fax: 1 441 236 5528

CARIBBEAN (ST LUCIA)

Mago Estate Hotel

PO Box 247, Soufriere, St Lucia
Tel: 1 758 459 5880
Fax: 1 758 459 7352

BERMUDA (PAGET)

Harmony Club All Inclusive

PO Box 299, South Shore Road, Paget,
Bermuda
Tel: 1 441 236 3500
Fax: 1 441 236 2624

CARIBBEAN (ST LUCIA)

**Windjammer Landing Villa
Beach Resort**

Labrelotte Bay Box 1504, Castries, St Lucia
Tel: 1 758 452 0913
Fax: 1 758 452 9454

BERMUDA (PAGET)

The Newstead Hotel

27 Harbour Road, Paget PG02, Bermuda
Tel: 1 9 441 236 6060
Fax: 1 9 441 236 7454

CARIBBEAN (ST VINCENT)

Camelot Inn

PO Box 787, Kingstown, St Vincent
Tel: 1 784 456 2100
Fax: 1 784 456 2233

BERMUDA (WARWICK)

Surf Side Beach Club

90 South Shore Rd, Warwick, Bermuda
Tel: 1 441 236 7100
Fax: 1 441 236 9765

CARIBBEAN (ST VINCENT)

Grand View Beach Hotel

Villa Point, Box 173, St Vincent, West
Indies
Tel: 1 784 458 4811
Fax: 1 784 457 4174

CANADA (SIDNEY)

**Seaside Luxury Resort Bed &
Breakfast**

8355 Lockside Drive, Sidney, British
Columbia, Canada
Tel: 1 250 544 1000
Fax: 1 250 544 1001

CARIBBEAN (TOBAGO)

Coco Reef Resort

Box 434, Scarborough, Tobago, West Indies
Tel: 1 868 639 8571
Fax: 1 868 639 8574

CARIBBEAN (ANGUILLA)

Frangipani Beach Club

Po Box 1378, Meads Bay, Anguilla, West
Indies
Tel: 1 264 497 6442
Fax: 1 264 497 6440

CARIBBEAN (TOBAGO)

Mount Irvine Bay Hotel

Box222 Mount Irvine Bay, Tobago
Tel: 1 868 639 8871
Fax: 1868 639 8800

CARIBBEAN (CURACAO)

Avila Beach Hotel

Penstraat 130, Willemstad, Curacao,
Antilles, West Indies
Tel: 599 9 461 4377
Fax: 599 9 461 1493

MEXICO (IXTAPA/ZIHUATANEJO)

Hotel Villa Del Sol

Playa La Ropa s/n, PO Box 84, Zihuatanejo,
Mexico
Tel: 52 755 4 2239
Fax: 52 755 4 2758

CARIBBEAN (DOMINICA)

Hummingbird Inn

Morne Daniel, Box 1901, Roseau, Dominica
Tel: 1 767 449 1042
Fax: 1 767 449 1042

ARIZONA (GREER)

Red Setter Inn and Cottage

8 Main Street, PO Box 133, Greer, Arizona
85927, USA
Tel: 1 888 994 7337
Fax: 1 520 735 7425

ARIZONA (PHOENIX)

Maricopa Manor

Box 7186, 15 West Pasadena Avenue,
Phoenix, Arizona 85013-2001, USA
Tel: 1 602 274 6302
Fax: 1 602 266 3904

ARIZONA (SEDONA)

Canyon Villa Inn

125 Canyon Circle Drive, Sedona, Arizona
86351, USA
Tel: 1 520 284 1226
Fax: 1 520 284 2114

ARIZONA (TUCSON)

White Stallion Ranch

9251 West Twin Peaks Road, Tucson,
Arizona 85743, USA
Tel: 1 520 297 0252
Fax: 1 520 744 2786

CALIFORNIA (CALISTOGA)

Cottage Grove Inn

1711 Lincoln Avenue, Calistoga, Califorua
94515, USA
Tel: 707 942 8400 or 800 799 2284
Fax: 1 702 942 2653

CALIFORNIA (FERNDALE)

Gingerbread Mansion Inn

400 Berding Street, (PO Box 40), Ferndale,
California 95536-0040, USA
Tel: 1 707 786 4000
Fax: 1 707 786 4381

CALIFORNIA (LA JOLLA)

The Bed & Breakfast Inn at La Jolla

7753 Draper Avenue, La Jolla, California
92037, USA
Tel: 1 858 456 2066
Fax: 1 858 456 1510

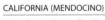

CALIFORNIA (MENDOCINO)

Joshua Grindle Inn

44800 Little Lake Road, PO Box 647,
Mendocino, California 95460, USA
Tel: 1 707 937 4143

CALIFORNIA (MUIR BEACH)

Pelican Inn

Highway 1, Muir Beach, California 94965,
USA
Tel: 1 415 383 6000
Fax: 1 415 383 3424

CALIFORNIA (NAPA VALLEY)

The Ink House

1575 Helena Highway at Whitehall Lane, St
Helena, California 94574-9775, USA
Tel: 1 707 963 3890
Fax: 1 707 968 0739

CALIFORNIA (NEVADA CITY)

Red Castle Inn Historic Lodging

109 Prospect Street, Nevada City, California
95959, USA
Tel: 1 530 265 5135
Fax: 1 530 265 3560

CALIFORNIA (PALM SPRINGS)

The Willows

412 West Tahquitz Canyon Way, Palm
Springs, California 92262, USA
Tel: 1 760 320 0771
Fax: 1 760 320 0780

CALIFORNIA (SAN FRANCISCO)

Nob Hill Lambourne

725 Pine Street, San Francisco, California
94108, USA
Tel: 1 415 433 2287
Fax: 1 415 433 0975

CALIFORNIA (SANTA ANA)

Woolley's Petite Suites

2721 Hotel Terrace Road, Santa Ana,
California 92705, USA
Tel: 1 714 540 1111
Fax: 1 714 662 1643

CALIFORNIA (SOLVANG)

The Alisal Guest Ranch & Resort

1054 Alisal Road, Solvang, California
93463, USA
Tel: 1 805 688 6411
Fax: 1 805 688 2510

COLORADO (DENVER)

Historic Castle Marne

1572 Race Street, Denver , Colorado 80206,
USA
Tel: 1 303 331 0621
Fax: 1 303 331 0623

COLORADO (STEAMBOAT SPRINGS)

Vista Verde Guest Ranch

Po Box 465, Steamboat Springs, Colorado
80477, USA
Tel: 1 970 879 3858
Fax: 1 970 879 1413

CONNECTICUT (GREENWICH)

The Homestead Inn

420 Fieldpoint Road, Greenwich,
Connecticut 06830, USA
Tel: 1 203 869 7500
Fax: 1 203 869 7502

CONNECTICUT (MYSTIC)

Stonecroft Country Inn

515 Pumpkin Hill Rd, Ledyard 06339, USA
Tel: 860 572 0771
Fax: 860 572 9161

DELAWARE (REHOBOTH BEACH)

Boardwalk Plaza Hotel

Olive Avenue & The Boardwalk, Rehoboth
Beach, Delaware 19971, USA
Tel: 1 302 227 7169
Fax: 1 302 227 0561

FLORIDA (HOLMES BEACH)

Harrington House

5626 Gulf Drive, Holmes Beach, Florida
34217, USA
Tel: 1 947 778 5444
Fax: 1 941 778 0527

FLORIDA (KEY WEST)

Island City House

411 William Street, Key West, Florida
33040, USA
Tel: 1 305 294 5702
Fax: 1 305 294 1289

FLORIDA (KEY WEST)

Simonton Court Historic Inn & Cottages

320 Simonton Street, Key West, Florida
33040, USA
Tel: 1 305 294 6386
Fax: 1 305 293 8446

FLORIDA (KEY WEST)

The Paradise Inn

819 Simonton Street, Key West, Florida
33040, USA
Tel: 305 293 8007
Fax: 305 293 0807

FLORIDA (MIAMI BEACH)

Hotel Ocean

1230-1238 Ocean Drive, Miami Beach,
Florida 33139, USA
Tel: 1 305 672 2579
Fax: 1 305 672 7665

GEORGIA (LITTLE ST SIMONS ISLAND)

The Lodge on Little St. Simons Island

PO Box 21078, St Simons Island, Georgia
31522-0578, USA
Tel: 1 912 638 7472
Fax: 1 912 634 1811

GEORGIA (PERRY)

Henderson Village

125 South Langston Circle, Perry, Georgia
31069, USA
Tel: 1 912 988 8696
Fax: 1 912 988 9009

GEORGIA (SAVANNAH)

The Eliza Thompson House

5 West Jones Street, Savannah, Georgia
31401, USA
Tel: 1 912 236 3620
Fax: 1 912 238 1920

GEORGIA (SAVANNAH)

Granite Steps

126 East Gaston Street, Savannah, Georgia
31401, USA
Tel: +1 912 233 5380
Fax: +1 912 236 3116

GEORGIA (SAVANNAH)

Magnolia Place Inn

503 Whittaker Street, Savannah, Georgia
31401, USA
Tel: 1 912 236 7674
Fax: 1 912 236 1145

GEORGIA (SAVANNAH)

Presidents Quarters

225 East President Street, Savannah,
Georgia 31401, USA
Tel: 1 912 233 1600
Fax: 1 912 238 0849

HAWAII (KAILUA-KONA)

Kailua Plantation House

75-5948 Alii Drive, Kailua-Kona, Hawaii
96740, USA
Tel: 1 808 329 3727
Fax: 1 808 326 7323

LOUISIANA (NEW ORLEANS)

Windsor Court

300 Gravier Street, New Orleans, Louisiana
70130, USA
Tel: 1 504 523 6000
Fax: 1 504 596 4513

MAINE (GREENVILLE)

The Lodge at Moosehead Lake

Upon Lily Bay Road, Box 1167, Greenville,
Maine 04441, USA
Tel: 1 207 695 4400
Fax: 1 207 695 2281

MAINE (LINCOLNSVILLE)

Inn at Oceans Edge

Route 1, Lincolnville, Maine 04843, USA
Tel: +1 207 236 0945
Fax: +1 207 236 0609

MARYLAND (TANEYTOWN)

Antrim 1844

30 Trevanion Road, Taneytown, Maryland
21787, USA
Tel: 1 410 756 6812
Fax: 1 410 756 2744

MASSACHUSETTS (BOSTON)

A Cambridge House

2218 Massachusetts Avenue, Cambridge,
Massachusetts 02140-1836, USA
Tel: 1 617 491 6300
Fax: 1 617 868 2848

MASSACHUSETTS (BOSTON)

Charles Street Inn

94 Charles Street, Boston, Massachusetts
02114 4643, USA
Tel: +1 617 371 0008
Fax: +1 617 371 0009

MASSACHUSETTS (CAPE COD)

Wedgewood Inn

83 Main Street, Route 6A, Yarmouth Port,
Massachusetts 02675, USA
Tel: 1 508 362 5157
Fax: 1 508 362 5851

MASSACHUSETTS (CHATHAM)

The Captain's House Inn

369-377 Old Harbor Road, Chatham, Cape
Cod, Massachusetts 02633, USA
Tel: 1 508 945 0127
Fax: 1 508 945 0866

MASSACHUSETTS (CHATHAM)

Chatham Town House Inn

11 Library Lane, Chatham, Massachusetts
02633, USA
Tel: 508 945-2180
Fax: 508 945-3990

MASSACHUSETTS (CHATHAM)

Pleasant Bay Village Resort

PO Box 772, Route 28, Chatham,
Massachusetts 02633, USA
Tel: 1 508 945 1133
Fax: 1 508 945 9701

MASSACHUSETTS (EASTHAM)

The Whalewalk Inn

220 Bridge Road, Eastham, Massachusetts
02642, USA
Tel: 1 508 255 0617
Fax: 1 508 240 0017

MASSACHUSETTS (LENOX)

Wheatleigh

Hawthorne Road, Lenox, Massachusetts
01240, USA
Tel: 1 413 637 0610
Fax: 1 413 637 4507

MASSACHUSETTS (MARTHA'S VINEYARD)

Colonial Inn

North Water Street, Edgartown,
Massachusetts 02539, USA
Tel: 1 508 627 4711
Fax: 1 508 627 5904

MASSACHUSETTS (ROCKPORT)

Seacrest Manor

99 Marmion Way, Rockport, Massachusetts
01966, USA
Tel: 1 978 546 2211

MICHIGAN (PETOSKEY)

Staffords Perry Hotel

Bay at Lewis Street, Petoskey, Michigan
49770, USA
Tel: 1 231 347 5492
Fax: 1 231 347 3413

MISSISSIPPI (BILOXI)

Father Ryan House

1196 Beach Boulevard, Biloxi, Mississippi
39530, USA
Tel: 1 228 435 1189
Fax: 1 228 436 3063

MISSISSIPPI (JACKSON)

Fairview Inn

734 Fairview Street, Jackson, Mississippi
39202, USA
Tel: 1 601 948 3429
Fax: 1 601 948 1203

MISSISSIPPI (VICKSBURG)

The Duff Green Mansion

1114 1st East Street, Vicksburg , Mississippi
39180, USA
Tel: 1 601 636 6968
Fax: 1 601 661 0079

NEW HAMPSHIRE (BETHLEHEM)

Adair

80 Guider Lane, Bethlehem, New
Hampshire 03574, USA
Tel: 1 603 444 2600
Fax: 1 603 444 4823

NEW YORK (CAZENOVIA)

The Brewster Inn

6 Ledyard Avenue, Cazenovia, New York
13035, USA
Tel: 1 315 655 9232
Fax: 1 315 655 2130

NEW YORK (CLARENCE)

Asa Ransom House

10529 Main Street, Route 5, Clarence, New
York 14031-1684, USA
Tel: 1 716 759 2315
Fax: 1 716 759 2791

NEW YORK (EAST AURORA)

The Roycroft Inn

40 South Grove Street, East Aurora, New
York 14052, USA
Tel: 1 716 652 5552
Fax: 1 716 655 5345

NEW YORK (GENEVA)

Geneva On The Lake

1001 Lockland Rd, Rt 14 South, Geneva,
New York 14456, USA
Tel: +1 315 789 7190
Fax: +1 315 789 0322

NEW YORK (ITHACA)

Benn Conger Inn

206 West Cortland Street, Groton, New
York 13073, USA
Tel: 1 607 898 5817
Fax: 1 607 898 5818

NEW YORK (ITHICA)

William Henry Miller Inn

303 North Aurora Street, Ithaca, New York
14850, USA
Tel: +1 607 256 4553
Fax: +1 256 0092

NEW YORK (NEW YORK)

The Franklin

164 East 87th Street, New York, USA
Tel: 1 212 369 1000
Fax: 1 212 369 8000

NORTH CAROLINA (ROBBINSVILLE)

Snowbird Mountain Lodge

275 Santeetlah Rd, Robbinsville, North
Carolina 28771, USA
Tel: 1 828 479 3433 / 800 941 9290
Fax: 1 828 479 34 73

NORTH CAROLINA (TRYON)

Pine Crest

200 Pine Crest Lane, Tryon, North Carolina
28782, USA
Tel: 1 828 859 9135
Fax: 1 828 859 9135

NORTH CAROLINA (WAYNESVILLE)

The Swag Country Inn

2300 Swag Road, Waynesville, North
Carolina 28786, USA
Tel: 1 828 926 0430
Fax: 1 828 926 2036

RHODE ISLAND (NEWPORT)

Castle Hill Inn and Resort

Ocean Drive, Newport, Rhode Island 02840, USA
Tel: 1 401 849 3800
Fax: 1 409 849 3898

RHODE ISLAND (NEWPORT)

The Inn at Shadow Lawn

120 Mantonomi Avenue, Newport, Rhode Island 02842, USA
Tel: 1 401 847 0902 or 800 352 3750
Fax: 1 401 848 6529

RHODE ISLAND (NEWPORT)

Vanderbilt Hall

41 Mary Street, Newport, Rhode Island 02840, USA
Tel: 1 401 846 6200
Fax: 1 401 846 0701

SOUTH CAROLINA (CHARLESTON)

Fulton Lane Inn

202 King Street, Charleston, South Carolina 29401, USA
Tel: 1 803 720 2600
Fax: 1 803 720 2940

SOUTH CAROLINA (PAWLEYS ISLAND)

Litchfield Plantation

Kings River Road, Pawleys Island, South Carolina 29585, USA
Tel: 1 843 237 9121
Fax: 1 843 237 1041

TENNESSEE (KINGSTON)

Whitestone Country Inn

1200 Paint Rock Road, Kingston, Tennessee 37763, USA
Tel: 1 865 376 0113
Fax: 1 865 376 4454

VERMONT (CHITTENDEN)

Tulip Tree Inn

49 Dam Road, Chittenden, Vermont 05737, USA
Tel: 1 802 483 6213
Fax: 1 802 483 2623

VERMONT (MANCHESTER VILLAGE)

1811 House

PO Box 39, Route 7A, Manchester Village, Vermont 05254, USA
Tel: 1 802 362 1811
Fax: 1 802 362 2443

VERMONT (NEWFANE)

Four Columns Inn

Po Box 278, Newfane, Vermont 05345, USA
Tel: 1 802 365 7713
Fax: 1 802 365 0022

VERMONT (STOWE)

The Mountain Road Resort

PO Box 8, 1007 Mountain Road, Stowe, Vermont 05672, USA
Tel: 1 802 253 4566
Fax: 1 802 253 7397

VERMONT (WEST TOWNSHEND)

Windham Hill Inn

West Townshend, Vermont 05359, USA
Tel: 1 802 874 4080
Fax: 1 802 874 4702

VERMONT (WESTON)

The Inn at Weston

Scenic Route100, Weston, Vermont 05161, USA
Tel: 1 802 824 6789
Fax: 1 802 824 3073

VIRGINIA (CHARLOTTESVILLE)

Clifton-The Country Inn & Estate

1296 Clifton Inn Drive, Charlottesville, Virginia 22941, USA
Tel: 1 804 971 1800
Fax: 1 804 971 7098

VIRGINIA (MIDDLEBURG)

The Goodstone Inn and Estate

36205 Snake Hill Rd, Middleburg, Virginia 20117, USA
Tel: 1540 687 4645
Fax: 1540 687 6115

WASHINGTON (ORCAS ISLAND)

Turtleback Farm Inn

1981 Crow Valley Road, Eastsound, Washington 98245, USA
Tel: 1 360 376 4914
Fax: 1 360 376 5329

WYOMING (CHEYENNE)

Nagle Warren Mansion B & B

222 E.17th Street, Cheyenne, Wyoming 82001, USA
Tel: 1 307 637 3333
Fax: 1 307 638 6879

MINI LISTINGS
Johansens Recommended Hotels & Lodges – Australia, New Zealand, The Pacific 2001
Here in brief are the entries that appear in full in Johansens Recommended Hotel & Lodges – Australia, New Zealand, The Pacific 2001.
To order Johansens guides turn to the order forms at the back of this book.

NEW SOUTH WALES (BRAIDWOOD)

The Doncaster Inn

Wilson Street, Braidwood, New South
Wales 2622, Australia
Tel: +61 2 4842 2356
Fax: +61 2 4842 2521

NEW SOUTH WALES (BUNDANOON)

Oaks Court Country House

Ross Street, Bundanoon, New South Wales
2578, Australia
Tel: +61 2 4883 6858
Fax: +61 2 4883 6196

NEW SOUTH WALES (HARDY'S BAY)

Headlands, Broken Bay

Po Box 10, Hardy's Bay, New South Wales
2257, Australia
Tel: +61 2 4360 1933
Fax: +61 2 4360 2013

NEW SOUTH WALES (SYDNEY)

The Harbour Rocks Hotel

34-52 Harrington Street, Sydney, New
South Wales 2000, Australia
Tel: +61 2 9251 8944
Fax: +61 2 9251 8900

NEW SOUTH WALES (TOOWOON BAY)

Kims Beachside Retreat

16 Charlton Street, Toowoon Bay, New
SouthWales 2261, Australia
Tel: +61 2 4332 1566
Fax: +61 2 4333 1544

NEW SOUTH WALES (ULLADULLA)

Ulladulla Guest House

39 Burrill Street, Ulladulla, New South
Wales 2539, Australia
Tel: +61 2 4455 1796
Fax: +61 2 4454 4660

NEW SOUTH WALES (WENTWORTH FALLS)

Whispering Pines

178-186 Falls Rd, Wentworth Falls, New
South Wales 2782, Australia
Tel: +61 2 4757 1449
Fax: +61 2 4757 1219

AUSTRALIAN CAPITAL TERITTORY (CANBERRA)

The York Canberra

31 Giles Street, Kingston, Canberra,
Austalian Capital Territory 2604, Australia
Tel: +61 2 6295 2333
Fax: +61 2 6295 9559

QUEENSLAND (BLOOMFIELD)

Bloomfield Rainforest Lodge

PO Box 966, Cairns, Queensland 4870,
Australia
Tel: +61 7 4035 9166
Fax: +61 7 4035 9180

QUEENSLAND (ATHERTON TABLELANDS)

Bracken Ridge Lodge

65 Vance Close, Yungaburra, Atherton
Tablelands, Queensland 4872, Australia
Tel: +61 7 4095 3421
Fax: +61 7 4095 3461

QUEENSLAND (DAINTREE)

Daintree Eco Lodge and Spa

20 Daintree Rd, Daintree, Queensland 4873,
Australia
Tel: +61 7 4098 6100
Fax: +61 7 4098 6200

QUEENSLAND (FRASER ISLAND)

Kingfisher Bay Resort and Village

Fraser Island, Urangan, Queensland 4655,
Australia
Tel: +61 7 4120 3333
Fax: +61 7 4127 9333

QUEENSLAND (GREEN ISLAND)

Green Island Resort

Po Box 898, Cairns, Queensland 4870,
Australia
Tel: +61 7 4031 3300
Fax: +61 7 4052 1511

QUEENSLAND (MONTVILLE)

The Falls B&B & Rainforest Cottages

20 Kondalilla Falls Road, Montville,
Queensland 4560, Australia
Tel: +61 7 5445 7000
Fax: +61 7 5445 7001

QUEENSLAND (PLANET DOWNS)

Planet Downs

Outback, Queensland, Australia
Tel: +61 7 3265 5022
Fax: +61 7 3265 3978

QUEENSLAND (SPRINGBROOK)

Springbrook Mountain Manor

2814 Springbrook Rd, Springbrook,
Queensland 4213, Australia
Tel: +61 7 5533 5344
Fax: +61 7 5533 5344

QUEENSLAND (WHITSUNDAY)

Laguna Quays

Kunapipi Springs Road, Whitsunday,
Queensland 4800, Australia
Tel: +61 7 4947 7777
Fax: +61 7 4949 7770

SOUTH AUSTRALIA (ADELAIDE-THORNGATE)

Myoora Heritage Accommodation

4 Carter Street, Thorngate, Adelaide, South
Australia 5082, Australia
Tel: +61 8 8344 2599
Fax: +61 8 8344 9575

SOUTH AUSTRALIA (ADELAIDE-STIRLING)

Thorngrove Manor

2 Glenside Lane, Stirling, Adelaide, South
Australia 5152, Australia
Tel: +61 8 8339 6748
Fax: +61 8 8370 9950

SOUTH AUSTRALIA (SEVENHILL-CLARE VALLEY)

Thorn Park Country House

College Road, Sevenhill, Clare Valley,
South Australia 5453, Australia
Tel: +61 8 8843 4304
Fax: +61 8 8843 4296

VICTORIA (BEECHWORTH)

Beechworth House

5 Dingle Road, Beechworth, Victoria 3747,
Australia
Tel: +61 3 5728 2817
Fax: +61 3 5728 2737

VICTORIA (EILDON)

Eucalypt Ridge

564 Skyline Road, Eildon, Victoria 3713,
Australia
Tel: +61 3 5774 2033
Fax: +61 3 5774 2610

VICTORIA (HALLS GAP-GRAMPIANS)

Marwood

Mount Zero Rd, Halls Gap, Victoria 3381,
Australia
Tel: +61 3 5356 4231
Fax: +61 3 5356 4513

VICTORIA (KALORAMA - MT DANDENONG)

Grey Gables

3 Grange Rd, Kalorama, Victoria 3766,
Australia
Tel: +61 3 9761 8609
Fax: +61 3 9728 8033

VICTORIA (LAKES ENTRANCE)

Deja Vu

17 Clara Street, Lakes Entrance, Victoria
3909, Australia
Tel: +61 3 5155 4330
Fax: +61 3 5155 3718

VICTORIA (MELBOURNE)

Hotel Lindrum

26 Flinders Street, Melbourne, Victoria
3000, Australia
Tel: +61 3 9668 1111
Fax: +61 3 9668 1199

VICTORIA (MOOROODUC)

Woodman Estate

136 Graydens Road, Moorooduc, Victoria
3933, Australia
Tel: +61 3 5978 8455
Fax: +61 3 5978 8522

VICTORIA (MOUNT BEAUTY)

Dreamers Mountain Accommodation

Kiewa Valley Highway, Tawonga South,
Mount Beauty, Victoria 3699, Australia
Tel: +61 3 5754 1222
Fax: +61 3 5754 1333

VICTORIA (PHILLIP ISLAND)

The Castle-Villa by the Sea

7-9 Steele Street, Cowes, Phillip Island,
Victoria 3922, Australia
Tel: +61 3 5952 1228
Fax: +61 3 5952 3926

VICTORIA (RED HILL)

Lindenderry at Red Hill

142 Arthurs Seat Rd, Red Hill, Victoria
3937, Australia
Tel: +61 3 5989 2933
Fax: +61 3 5989 2936

VICTORIA (ROMSEY)

Cope-Williams Winery

Glenfern Rd, Romsey, Victoria 3434,
Australia
Tel: +61 3 5429 5428
Fax: +61 3 5429 5655

VICTORIA (TORQUAY)

Freshwater Green Country House

3 Jetti Lane, Torquay, Victoria 3228,
Australia
Tel: +61 3 5261 3366
Fax: +61 3 5261 9266

VICTORIA (YARRA VALLEY)

Chateau Yering

Melba Highway, Yering, Yarra Valley,
Victoria 3770, Australia
Tel: +61 3 9237 3333
Fax: +61 3 9237 3300

WESTERN AUSTRALIA (BROOME)

McAlpine House

84 Herbert Street, Broome, Western
Australia 6725, Australia
Tel: +61 8 9192 3886
Fax: +61 8 9192 3887

WESTERN AUSTRALIA (BROOME)

North Star Charters

PO Box 654, Shop 2, 25 Carnarvon Street,
Broome, Western Australia 6725, Australia
Tel: +61 8 9192 1829
Fax: +61 8 9192 1830

WESTERN AUSTRALIA (PERTH)

Joondalup Resort

Country Club Boulevard, Joondalup, Perth,
Western Australia 6027, Australia
Tel: +61 8 9400 8888
Fax: +61 8 9400 8889

COOK ISLANDS (AITUTAKI)

Aitutaki Pearl Beach Resort

PO Box 99, Aitutaki, Cook Islands
Tel: +682 31 201
Fax: +682 31 202

COOK ISLANDS (RAROTONGA)

Crown Beach Resort

PO Box 47, Rarotonga, Cook Islands
Tel: +682 23 953
Fax: +682 23 951

COOK ISLANDS (RAROTONGA)

Rarotongan Beach Resort

Po Box 103, Rarotonga, Cook Islands
Tel: +682 25 800
Fax: +682 25 799

FIJI ISLANDS (LAUTOKA)

Blue Lagoon Cruises

183 Vitogo Parade, Lautoka, Fiji Islands
Tel: +679 661 622
Fax: +679 664 098

FIJI ISLANDS (MAMANUCA ISLANDS)

Tokoriki Island Resort

PO Box 10547, Nadi Airport, Nadi, Fiji
Islands
Tel: +679 725 474
Fax: +679 725 928

FIJI ISLANDS (MATANGI ISLAND)

Matangi Island Resort

Matangi Island, Fiji Islands
Tel: +679 880 260
Fax: +679 880 274

FIJI ISLANDS (SAVUSAVU)

Namale Resort

PO Box 244, Savusavu, Fiji Islands
Tel: +679 850 435
Fax: +679 850 400

FIJI ISLANDS (TAVEUNI ISLAND)

Taveuni Island Resort

Taveuni Island, Fiji Islands
Tel: +679 880 441
Fax: +679 880 466

FIJI ISLANDS (TOBERUA ISLAND)

Toberua Island Resort

GPO Box 567, Suva, Fiji Islands
Tel: +679 302 356
Fax: +679 302 215

FIJI ISLANDS (YASAWA ISLANDS)

Turtle Island, Fiji

Yasawa Islands, PO Box 9371 Nadi Airport,
Nadi, Fiji Islands
Tel: +61 3 9618 1100
Fax: +61 3 9618 1199

FIJI ISLANDS (YASAWA ISLANDS)

Yasawa Island Resort

PO Box 10128, Nadi Airport, Nadi, Fiji
Islands
Tel: +679 722 266
Fax: +679 724 456

NORTH ISLAND (AUCKLAND)

Aachen House Boutique Hotel

39 Market Rd, Remuera, Auckland, New
Zealand
Tel: +64 9 520 2329
Fax: +64 9 524 2898

NORTH ISLAND (GISBORNE)

Acton Estate

577 Back Ormond Road, Gisborne, New
Zealand
Tel: +64 6 867 9999
Fax: +64 6 867 1116

NORTH ISLAND (HAWKES BAY - HAVELOCK NORTH)

Mangapapa Lodge

466 Napier Rd, Havelock North, Hawkes
Bay, New Zealand
Tel: +64 6 878 3234
Fax: +64 6 878 1214

NORTH ISLAND (ROTORUA)

Treetops Lodge

Koaroha Road, Horohoro, Rotorua, New
Zealand
Tel: +64 9 579 1187
Fax: +64 9 579 7421

NORTH ISLAND (RUSSELL-BAY OF ISLANDS)

Kimberley lodge

Pitt Street , PO Box 166, Russell, Bay of
Island, New Zealand
Tel: +64 9 403 7090
Fax: +64 9 403 7239

NORTH ISLAND (KERIKERI - BAY OF ISLANDS)

Villa Maria Petit Hotel

Inlet Road, PO Box 230, Kerikeri, Bay of
Islands, New Zealand
Tel: +64 9 407 9311
Fax: +64 9 407 9311

NORTH ISLAND (PAUANUI BEACH)

Puka Park Resort

Private Bag, Pauanui Beach 2850, New
Zealand
Tel: +64 7 864 8088
Fax: +64 7 864 8112

NORTH ISLAND (ROTORUA)

Kawaha Point Lodge

171 Kawaha Point Road, Rotorua, New
Zealand
Tel: +64 7 346 3602
Fax: +64 7 346 3671

NORTH ISLAND (ROTORUA)

Solitaire Lodge

Lake Tarawera, Rotorua RD5, New Zealand
Tel: +64 7 362 8208
Fax: +64 7 362 8445

NORTH ISLAND (TAUPO)

Lake Taupo Lodge

41 Mapara Road, Acacia Road, Taupo, New
Zealand
Tel: +64 7 378 7386
Fax: +64 7 377 3226

NORTH ISLAND (TAUPO)

The Pillars

7 Deborah Rise, Bonshaw Park, Taupo, New
Zealand
Tel: +64 7 378 1512
Fax: +64 7 378 1511

NORTH ISLAND (TAURANGA)

Tinopai Lodge

20 Tinopai Drive, Tauranga, New Zealand
Tel: +64 7 548 1515
Fax: +64 7 548 1525

NORTH ISLAND (WAIKATO)

Brooklands Country Estate

RD1, Ngaruawahia, Waikato, New Zealand
Tel: +64 7 825 4756
Fax: +64 7 825 4873

NORTH ISLAND (WHANGAMATA)

Bushland Park

444 Wentworth Valley Road, Whangamata,
New Zealand
Tel: +64 7 865 7468
Fax: +64 7 865 7486

NORTH ISLAND (WHITIANGA)

Villa Toscana Lodge

Ohuka Park, Rimu Street, Whitianga, New
Zealand
Tel: +64 7 866 2293
Fax: +64 7 866 2269

SOUTH ISLAND (CASS)

Grasmere Lodge High Country Retreat

State Highway 73, Cass, Canterbury, New
Zealand
Tel: +64 3 318 8407
Fax: +64 3 318 8263

SOUTH ISLAND (CHRISTCHURCH)

The Charlotte Jane

110 Papanui Road, Merivale, Christchurch,
New Zealand
Tel: +64 3 355 1028
Fax: +64 3 355 8882

SOUTH ISLAND (DARFIELD)

Bangor Country Estate

Bangor Road, Darfield, New Zealand
Tel: +64 3 318 7588
Fax: +64 3 318 8485

SOUTH ISLAND (DUNEDIN)

Corstorphine House

23 Milburn Street, Dunedin, New Zealand
Tel: +64 3 487 6676
Fax: +64 3 487 6672

SOUTH ISLAND (MARLBOROUGH - BLENHEIM)

The Old St Mary's Convent

776 Rapaura Rd, Blenheim, Marlborough,
New Zealand
Tel: +64 3 570 5700
Fax: +64 3 570 5700

SOUTH ISLAND (NELSON)

The Lodge at Paratiho Farms

545 Waiwhero Rd, Rd 2 Upper Moutere,
Motueka, Nelson, New Zealand
Tel: +64 3 528 2100
Fax: +64 3 528 2101

SOUTH ISLAND (MURCHISON-LAKE ROTOROA)

Lake Rotoroa Lodge

RD3 Lake Rotoroa, Murchison, New
Zealand
Tel: +64 3 523 9121
Fax: +64 3 523 9028

SOUTH ISLAND (NELSON)

Cathedral Inn

369 Trafalgar Street South, Nelson, New
Zealand
Tel: +64 3 548 7369
Fax: +64 3 548 0369

SOUTH ISLAND (QUEENSTOWN)

Manata Lodge

111 Tucker Beach Road, Queenstown, New
Zealand
Tel: +64 3 442 3440
Fax: +64 3 442 3110

SOUTH ISLAND(QUEENSTOWN)

Matakauri Lodge

Glenorchy Rd, Queenstown, New Zealand
Tel: +64 3 441 1008
Fax: +64 3 441 2180

SOUTH ISLAND (QUEENSTOWN)

White Shadows Country Inn

58 Hunter Road, Queenstown, New Zealand
Tel: +64 3 442 0871
Fax: +64 3 442 0872

SOUTH ISLAND (RANGIORA)

Serenada Country Lodge

Food Hills Road, Rangiora, New Zealand
Tel: +64 3 313 2263
Fax: +64 3 313 2264

SOUTH ISLAND (WAIPANA)

Mountford Vineyard

431 Omihi Road, Waipara, North
Canterbury, New Zealand
Tel: +64 3 314 6819
Fax: +64 3 314 6820

PREFERRED PARTNERS

Preferred partners are those organisations specifically chosen and exclusively recommended by Johansens for the quality and excellence of their products and services for the mutual benefit of Johansens recommendations, readers and independent travellers. For further details, please contact Fiona Patrick at Johansens on 0207 566 9700.

ORDER FORM

order 3 titles get £5 off • order 4 titles get £10 off • order 5 titles get £20 off

or you can order the Chairman's collection and save £35

Simply indicate the quantity of each title you wish to order, total up the cost and then make your appropriate discount. Complete your order below and choose your preferred method of payment. Then send it to Johansens, FREEPOST (CB 264), 43 Millharbour, London E14 9BR (no stamp required). FREE gifts will automatically be dispatched with your order. Fax orders welcome on 0207 537 3594.

ALTERNATIVELY YOU CAN ORDER IMMEDIATELY ON FREEPHONE 0800 269 397 and quote ref   B16

Recommended Hotels - Great Britain & Ireland 2001
Publication date: October 2000

I wish to order
QUANTITY
copy/ies priced at £19.95 each.
Total cost
£

Recommended Country Houses - Great Britain & Ireland 2001
Publication date: October 2000

I wish to order
QUANTITY
copy/ies priced at £11.95 each.
Total cost
£

Recommended Traditional Inns, Hotels & Restaurants - Great Britain 2001
Publication date: October 2000

I wish to order
QUANTITY
copy/ies priced at £11.95 each.
Total cost
£

Historic Houses, Castles & Gardens 2001 (incorporating Museums & Galleries)
Publication date: December 2000

I wish to order
QUANTITY
copy/ies priced at £7.95 each.
Total cost
£

Recommended Hotels - Europe & The Mediterranean 2001
Publication date: October 2000

I wish to order
QUANTITY
copy/ies priced at £16.95 each.
Total cost
£

Recommended Hotels - North America, Bermuda & The Caribbean 2001
Publication date: October 2000

I wish to order
QUANTITY
copy/ies priced at £12.95 each.
Total cost
£

Recommended Hotels, Country Houses & Game Lodges – Southern Africa, Mauritius, The Seychelles 2001 Publ. date: October 2000

I wish to order
QUANTITY
copy/ies priced at £9.95 each.
Total cost
£

Recommended Hotels & Lodges Australia, New Zealand, The Pacific 2001
Publication date: October 2000

NEW

I wish to order
QUANTITY
copy/ies priced at £9.95 each.
Total cost
£

Recommended Business Meeting Venues 2001
Publication date: February 2001

I wish to order
QUANTITY
copy/ies priced at £25.00 each.
Total cost
£

Johansens Pocket Guide 2001
Publication date: January 2001

NEW

I wish to order
QUANTITY
copy/ies priced at £7.95 each.
Total cost
£

The Chairman's Collection

**order the complete collection of Johansens Recommended Guides
for only £99.55 a saving of £35
PLUS FREE P&P worth £4.50
PLUS FREE Luxury Luggage Tag worth £15
PLUS FREE Privilege Card worth £20**

The Chairman's Collection contains the following titles:
•Business Meetings Venues •Traditional Inns, Hotels & Restaurants - GB •Hotels - GB & Ireland •Country Houses - GB & Ireland •Historic Houses, Castles & Gardens •Hotels, Country Houses & Game Lodges - Southern Africa •Hotels - North America, Bermuda, The Caribbean •Hotels - Europe & The Mediterranean •Hotels & Lodges - Australia, New Zealand, The Pacific • Johansens Pocket Guide 2001

Now please complete your order and payment details

I have ordered 3 titles - £5 off   −£5.00

I have ordered 4 titles - £10 off   −£10.00

I have ordered 5 titles - £20 off   −£20.00

Total cost of books ordered minus discount
(not including the Chairman's Collection)   £

Privilege Card - FREE WITH ANY ORDER
Additional cards can be ordered for £20   £

**Luxury Luggage Tag - Johansens branded polished
steel tag at £15. Quantity and total cost:**   £

POSTAGE & PACKING
(UK) for a single item add £2.50
More than one item add £4.50
(Outside) UK for a single item add £4.00
More than one item add £6.00   £

I wish to order the Chairman's collection at £99.55
(no P&P required) Enter quantity and total cost: £

**Johansens Gold Blocked SLIP CASE at £5 for the
Chairman's Collection. Quantity and total cost:**   £

GRAND TOTAL   £

I have chosen my Johansens Guides and (please tick)

I enclose a cheque payable to Johansens ☐
I enclose my order on company letterheading, please invoice (UK only) ☐
Please note that books will be sent upon payment being received
Please debit my credit/charge card account (please tick) ☐

☐ MasterCard   ☐ Amex   ☐ Visa   ☐ Switch (Issue Number) ▢

Card Holders Name (Mr/Mrs/Miss)

Address

Postcode

Telephone

Card No.

Exp Date

Signature

**NOW simply detach the order form and send it to Johansens,
FREEPOST (CB264), 43 Millharbour, London E14 9BR** (no stamp required)
FREE gifts will be dispatched with your order. Fax orders welcome on 0207 537 3594

GUEST SURVEY REPORT

Your own Johansens 'inspection' gives reliability to our guides and assists in the selection of Award Nominations

Name of Hotel: _____

Location of Hotel: _____

Page No: _____

Date of visit: _____

Name of GUEST: _____

Address of GUEST: _____

_____Postcode _____

Please tick one box in each category below:	Excellent	Good	Disappointing	Poor
Bedrooms				
Public Rooms				
Restaurant/Cuisine				
Service				
Welcome/Friendliness				
Value For Money				

Occasionally we may allow other reputable organisations to write with offers which may be of interest. If you prefer not to hear from them, tick this box ☐

To: Johansens, c/o Norwood Mailing CO Ltd, FREEPOST CB264, London SE27 0BR